KV-512-413

Contents

Chapter 1: Vaping: Overview

Chapter 2: Risks

Chapter 3: What next?

Introduction

Vaping is Volume 428 in the **issues** series. The aim of the series is to offer current, diverse information about important issues in our world, from a UK perspective.

About Vaping

9% of school children aged 11 to 15-years-old vape on a regular or occasional basis. This book looks at the reasons for the rise in under-age vaping. It also considers the health risks, addictive nature, and environmental impact of vape and e-cigarette use.

Our sources

Titles in the **issues** series are designed to function as educational resource books, providing a balanced overview of a specific subject.

The information in our books is comprised of facts, articles and opinions from many different sources, including:

- Newspaper reports and opinion pieces
- Website factsheets
- Magazine and journal articles
- Statistics and surveys
- Government reports
- Literature from special interest groups.

A note on critical evaluation

Because the information reprinted here is from a number of different sources, readers should bear in mind the origin of the text and whether the source is likely to have a particular bias when presenting information (or when conducting their research). It is hoped that, as you read about the many aspects of the issues explored in this book, you will critically evaluate the information presented.

It is important that you decide whether you are being presented with facts or opinions. Does the writer give a biased or unbiased report? If an opinion is being expressed, do you agree with the writer? Is there potential bias to the 'facts' or statistics behind an article?

Activities

Throughout this book, you will find a selection of assignments and activities designed to help you engage with the articles you have been reading and to explore your own opinions. Some tasks will take longer than others and there is a mixture of design, writing and research-based activities that you can complete alone or in a group.

Further research

At the end of each article we have listed its source and a website that you can visit if you would like to conduct your own research. Please remember to critically evaluate any sources that you consult and consider whether the information you are viewing is accurate and unbiased.

Issues Online

The **issues** series of books is complemented by our online resource, issuesonline.co.uk

On the Issues Online website you will find a wealth of information, covering over 70 topics, to support the PSHE and RSE curriculum.

Why Issues Online?

Researching a topic? Issues Online is the best place to start for...

Librarians

Issues Online is an essential tool for librarians: feel confident you are signposting safe, reliable, user-friendly online resources to students and teaching staff alike. We provide multi-user concurrent access, so no waiting around for another student to finish with a resource. Issues Online also provides FREE downloadable posters for your shelf/wall/table displays.

Teachers

Issues Online is an ideal resource for lesson planning, inspiring lively debate in class and setting lessons and homework tasks.

Our accessible, engaging content helps deepen students' knowledge, promotes critical thinking and develops independent learning skills.

Issues Online saves precious preparation time. We wade through the wealth of material on the internet to filter the best quality, most relevant and up-to-date information you need to start exploring a topic.

Our carefully selected, balanced content presents an overview and insight into each topic from a variety of sources and viewpoints.

Students

Issues Online is designed to support your studies in a broad range of topics, particularly social issues relevant to young people today.

Thousands of articles, statistics and infographs instantly available to help you with research and assignments.

With 24/7 access using the powerful Algolia search system, you can find relevant information quickly, easily and safely anytime from your laptop, tablet or smartphone, in class or at home.

Visit issuesonline.co.uk to find out more!

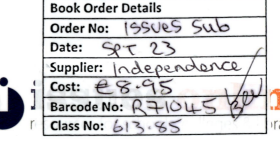

Nicotine vaping in England 2022 evidence update main findings

1. The review

This evidence review is the eighth in a series of independent reports on vaping originally commissioned by Public Health England and now by the Office for Health Improvement and Disparities in the Department of Health and Social Care.

This report was led by academics at King's College London with a group of international collaborators and is the most comprehensive to date. Its main focus is a systematic review of the evidence on the health risks of nicotine vaping.

2. Health risks

The report primarily looks at data on human exposure to vaping, complemented with findings from animal and cell studies. It provides the most robust evidence on health risks of vaping to date. It also assesses the relative risks of vaping compared with smoking, as well as the absolute risks of vaping compared with not vaping or smoking.

2.1 Overall conclusions

Based on the evidence that the team reviewed, the conclusions were that:

- in the short and medium term, vaping poses a small fraction of the risks of smoking

- vaping is not risk-free, particularly for people who have never smoked

- evidence is mostly limited to short and medium term effects and studies assessing longer term vaping (for more than 12 months) are necessary

- more standardised and consistent methodologies in future studies would improve interpretation of the evidence

2.2 Biomarkers of toxicant exposure

Biomarkers of toxicant exposure are measurements of potentially harmful substance levels in the body. The evidence reviewed suggests there is:

- significantly lower exposure to harmful substances from vaping compared with smoking, as shown by biomarkers associated with the risk of cancer, respiratory and cardiovascular conditions

- similar or higher exposure to harmful substances from vaping compared with not using nicotine products

- no significant increase of toxicant biomarkers after short-term secondhand exposure to vaping among people who do not smoke or vape

2.3 Biomarkers of potential harm

Biomarkers of potential harm are measurements of biological changes in the body due to an exposure to smoking or vaping. Although this review looked at many studies of biomarkers of potential harm, the team could draw only limited conclusions. However, better-run studies assessing short- and medium-term risks, found no major causes of concern associated with vaping.

3. Smoking and vaping prevalence

3.1 Young people

The latest data from the ASH-Youth 2022 survey of 11 to 18 year olds in England show that:

- current smoking prevalence (including occasional and regular smoking) is 6% in 2022, compared with 4.1% in 2021 and 6.7% in 2020

- current vaping prevalence (including occasional and regular vaping) is 8.6% in 2022, compared with 4% in 2021 and 4.8% in 2020

- most young people who have never smoked are also not currently vaping (98.3%)

- use of disposable vaping products has increased substantially, with 52.8% of current vapers using them in 2022, compared with 7.8% in 2021 and 5.3% in 2020

3.2 Adults

The latest data from several national studies of adults in England show that:

- smoking prevalence in England in 2021 was between 12.7% and 14.9% depending on the survey, which equates to between 5.6 and 6.6 million adults who smoke

- vaping prevalence in England in 2021 was between 6.9% and 7.1%, depending on the survey, which equates to between 3.1 and 3.2 million adults who vape

- vaping prevalence among adults who have never smoked remained very low, at between 0.6% and 0.7% in 2021

- the popularity of disposable vaping products has increased among adults who vape, with 15.2% using them in 2022 compared with 2.2% in 2021

- tank type products remained the most popular vaping devices (used by 64.3% of adult vapers in 2022)

- vaping products remain the most common aid used by people to help them stop smoking

- in stop smoking services in 2020 to 2021, quit attempts involving a vaping product were associated with the highest success rates (64.9% compared with 58.6% for attempts not involving a vaping product)

- the stop smoking service data are consistent with the latest evidence from the Cochrane Living Systematic Review on electronic cigarettes for smoking cessation which also shows vaping is effective for stopping smoking

4. Flavours

Fruit flavours remained the most popular among adults and young people who vape, followed by 'menthol/mint'.

Overall, there is a lack of evidence on whether flavourings affect health risks. Vaping products that contain the flavouring chemical cinnamaldehyde are a cause of concern, and regulatory bodies should review its use in e-liquids.

There is limited evidence that some flavourings in vaping products have the potential to alter cellular responses (from animal and cell studies), but less than exposure to tobacco smoke.

5. Nicotine

Vaping products generally provide lower nicotine levels to users than smoking does. However, people who are experienced vapers can achieve nicotine levels similar to people who smoke.

Existing evidence suggests that the risk and severity of nicotine dependency from vaping is lower than for smoking but varies by product characteristics (like device type and nicotine concentration in e-liquids). This is consistent with evidence on nicotine exposure from biomarker and pharmacokinetic studies from the current review.

6. Harm perceptions

In 2021, only 34% of adults who smoked accurately believed that vaping was less harmful than smoking. Only 11% of adults who smoked knew that none or a small amount of the risks of smoking were due to nicotine. Inaccurate perceptions need to be addressed.

The evidence reviewed also suggests that:

- people's perceptions about vaping harms can influence their subsequent vaping and smoking behaviour

- communicating accurate information about the relative harms of vaping can help to correct misperceptions of vaping, particularly among adults

Interventions on absolute harms of vaping that aim to deter young people need to be carefully designed so they do not misinform people (particularly smokers) about the relative harms of smoking and vaping.

29 September 2022

Key Facts

- Data collected from the ASH-Youth 2022 survey of 11-18 year olds in England show current vaping prevalence is 8.6% in 2022, compared with 4% in 2021 and 4.8% in 2020.

- The latest data from several national studies of adults in England shows that the popularity of disposable vaping products has increased among adults who vape to 15.2% in 2022 compared with 2.2% in 2021.

- Vaping products remain the most common aid used by people to help them stop smoking.

Research

Conduct a survey amongst your classmates and family members. How many of them smoke or vape? How many used to smoke but now vape instead? Produce a graph to show your findings.

www.gov.uk

Most Britons want to ban cigarettes – and half want to ban vaping products

By Christien Pheby

Most Britons want to ban cigarettes – including 38% who want to ban them immediately or in the next two years

Thinking about the sale of (cigarettes) in the UK, which of the following comes closest to your view? (%)

Their sale should be banned either immediately or in the very near future (e.g. within the next two years)	38
Their sale should be banned, but further into the future (e.g. from 2030)	19
There should not be a ban on their sale	32
Don't know	11

Source: YouGov 29-30 July 2021

Half of Brits want to see a ban on vaping products – now or in future

Thinking about the sale of [vaping products] in the UK, which of the following comes closest to your view? (%)

Their sale should be banned either immediately or in the very near future (e.g. within the next two years)	27
Their sale should be banned, but further into the future (e.g. from 2030)	21
There should not be a ban on their sale	36
Don't know	16

Source: YouGov 29-30 July 2021

The global tobacco firm Philip Morris International (PMI) recently announced its support for a nationwide ban on the sale of cigarettes within a decade. The Marlboro maker also indicated that it would withdraw its own cigarette brands from UK shelves in the same time frame.

It's a move that's broadly in tune with public sentiment: new polling from YouGov shows that close to three in five Britons (57%) support an outright ban on the sale of cigarettes, compared to a third (32%) who do not. And while one in five (19%) are in favour of a ban from 2030 onwards, two in five (38%) want the government to move even faster – outlawing these products either immediately or in the near future.

PMI CEO Jacek Olczak says that government action would 'end the confusion' around 'smoke-free alternatives' such as e-cigarettes, which the Benson & Hedges manufacturer will emphasise as it attempts to evolve into a 'healthcare and wellness' company.

But our research shows that Britons also tend to favour banning vaping products: a quarter (27%) of the public would remove them from sale as soon as possible, while a fifth (21%) would ban them from 2030 onwards. Overall, half are in favour of a nationwide vape escape (48%) – now or later – while just over a third are opposed (36%).

Along age lines, people in the 18-24 group are slightly more likely to favour outlawing cigarettes at some point (60%) and less likely to be in favour of allowing them to remain on sale (24%), while over-65s aren't far off general public opinion: 39% want to ban them now, 19% want them banned further in the future, and 32% don't want a ban at all. By contrast, older Britons are most supportive of a ban on vaping products: more than half (52%) of over-65s want to see them prohibited compared to 46% of 18-24s, with a third (32%) favouring an imminent ban compared to just a quarter (24%) of the youngest cohort.

While an outright ban on smoking and vaping may not be on the cards just yet, recent reports suggest that the government is considering raising the legal age of buying tobacco to 21 – and outlawing the sale of flavoured e-cigarettes entirely.

10 September 2021

www.yougov.co.uk

Vaping: is it good or bad?

By Carlota Pato

H on Lik was 47 years old when he developed the first modern e-cigarette. The year was 2003 and Lik, a heavy smoker, was struggling to quit. Using his knowledge of Chinese medicine and mechanics, Lik set out to create a product that would satisfy his sharp nicotine cravings without tobacco smoke, that is. Vapour was the key. Today, it is generally believed that vaping is not harmful – or at least, when compared to smoking – but to what extent is this true?

E-cigarette basics: what is vaping?

E-cigarettes, also called e-cigs or vapes, are small lithium battery-powered devices. Rather than burning tobacco leaves, e-cigarettes work by heating a liquid (known as e-liquid) until it turns into an aerosol (vapour). This aerosol is inhaled into the lungs and exhaled as a cloud into the air. Although the chemical compound of the e-liquid can vary, the typical combination includes: nicotine, for the buzz; vegetable glycerine, for the cloud of vapour; flavouring agents, for the taste and smell; propylene glycol, for the flavour to bind to; and other mixing agents that form the liquid – many of which have not yet been identified. Some e-cigarettes are available without nicotine.

Since 2003, the popularity of e-cigarettes has swept the global market, with use not only gaining traction among ex-smokers and smokers, but also among people experimenting with cigarette products for the first time. More than 4.3 million people use e-cigarettes in the UK alone. Of this figure, 2.4 million people are ex-smokers, 1.5 million people are current smokers and 350,000 people had never smoked a cigarette before taking up vaping. The reasons for vaping are far-reaching, from quitting smoking to having a cheaper alternative to regular cigarettes that doesn't smell as bad and tastes much better.

The silver bullet for smoking cessation?

E-cigarettes were originally designed to help smokers manage the transition from regular cigarette smoking to not smoking at all. Evidence over the years has shown that e-cigarettes may be as twice as effective as conventional smoking treatments. Working like nicotine replacement therapy, e-cigarettes can give vapers the nicotine hit they need to beat their cravings, but without exposing vapers to the toxic chemicals in tobacco smoke.

Switching to vaping can thus help to prevent more than 50 health conditions associated with regular cigarettes, including stroke, chronic obstructive pulmonary disease, and 15 different types of cancer.

In fact, e-cigarette aerosol generally contains fewer chemicals than regular cigarettes. This includes solid particles like smoke, which can be deposited deep in the bronchial tree of the lungs. Since there is no ignition involved, tar and carbon monoxide are also absent in e-cigarettes. These are two of the most harmful chemicals found in tobacco smoke. Although studies are limited, there is also no clear evidence so far that the secondhand vapour from e-cigarettes is harmful to the health of others. This compares to the dangers of secondhand smoke from regular cigarettes, which contains more than 4,000 irritants, carcinogens, and toxins, exposing others to the same health risks as smokers.

E-cigarette aerosol is not harmless 'water vapour'

Yet, while e-cigarettes can help smokers quit, vaping is not completely safe.

Nicotine, the main agent in e-cigarettes, is a highly addictive chemical. It causes intense urges and cravings, as well as withdrawal symptoms that can disrupt quality of life. Nicotine also stimulates the adrenal glands, which leads to the sudden release of adrenaline. This in turn can cause acute increases in blood pressure, heart rate and respiration, which raises the risk of suffering cardiovascular disease, hypertension, or a heart attack. Along with the physical perils, studies have shown that there are also cognitive risks linked to nicotine exposure in the developing brain, which does not fully form until the age of 25. This puts teenagers and young people who vape at risk. Inducing molecular activity, nicotine can harm the parts of the brain responsible for decision-making, memory, learning, and impulse control.

Most nicotine vaping products in the UK are covered by tight quality and safety regulations designed to protect vapers. This includes the banning of certain chemical compounds in e-liquid. Despite this, the wide range of e-liquids available means that vapers don't always know what chemical ingredients they are consuming in their e-cigarettes. Carcinogens (cancer-causing substances) and ultrafine particles have been found in e-cigarettes, for example, whilst some e-cigarettes marketed as being nicotine-free have actually been found to contain nicotine. Other e-cigarettes can even be modified to deliver higher substance dosages and recreational drugs, such as marijuana.

The heating process of e-cigarettes can also release new chemicals, including formaldehydes, a flammable gas linked to cancer in some studies. Other contaminants like nickel, tin, and aluminum have been found in e-cigarette aerosol as well, which worsen asthma and can potentially cause irreversible chronic lung diseases. One of these risks is the one caused by the flavourings that are used to infuse e-cigarette liquid. Although approved for ingestion, not all of these flavourings have been tested and considered safe for inhalation as aerosol. First-time vapers should especially look out for symptoms of cough, mouth and throat irritation, shortness of breath, and nausea. These may be the signs of e-cigarette associated lung disease.

Additionally, there are concerns that e-cigarettes (which simulate smoking) could act as a gateway to future tobacco cigarette consumption. A model in 2015 concluded that for 2,070 adult smokers who had quit that year through vaping, more than 167,000 teenage and young adult vapers had made the transition from e-cigarettes to regular cigarettes. In some cases, however, people choose not to do either, deciding to dual instead, which refers to the use of e-cigarettes while continuing to smoke regular cigarettes at the same time. Dual use increases the risk for heart attack by five times.

Cigarette users looking to quit

Overall, vaping is less harmful than smoking, but not risk-free. There is still a lot that remains unknown about e-cigarettes, including their exact chemical content, and while their use shows potential in helping smoking cessation, smokers wanting to quit will need to use conventional smoking treatments as well to be truly free of smoke.

The safest health option is to not use e-cigarettes at all.

15 December 2022

Teenagers vaping more in UK than most of Europe as ministers prepare clampdown

Government launch review to examine how e-cigarettes are advertised to young on social media and consider banning disposable flavoured vapes.

By Laura Donnelly, Health Editor

Britain has one of the highest levels of teen vaping in Western Europe, research shows, as ministers prepare to clamp down on e-cigarettes.

An international study of 35 countries shows that rates of vaping between those aged 15 and 24 are among the highest in comparable nations.

The research by the Organisation for Economic Co-operation and Development shows 7 per cent of those in this age group make regular use of e-cigarettes – compared with 1 per cent of those in Spain.

In Western Europe, rates were only higher in France, at 8.5 per cent, and the Netherlands, at 8.9 per cent.

Separate research by Ash, the anti-smoking charity, last year found the proportion of children aged 11 to 17 currently vaping jumped from 4 per cent in 2020 to 7 per cent in 2022.

In 2013, just 3 per cent of children aged 11 to 15 had ever vaped, but this rose to 8 per cent in 2020 and 10 per cent in 2022.

It comes as ministers prepare to consult on a clamp-down on vaping, to make it less appealing to children.

The Government is considering banning disposable flavoured vapes, with a review expected to examine the 'appearance and characteristics' of vaping products currently on sale.

The review is also set to examine the way they are branded and advertised over social media, amid concerns products are being deliberately targeted at youngsters.

Many experts have raised concerns that many of the products appeal to young sensibilities, with flavours like sweets and fruits.

In a speech early next month Neil O Brien, the public health minister, is expected to ask experts how to best to protect children from highly addictive nicotine.

It will also include a formal reply to an independent review by Dr Javed Khan which looked into the Government's goal to make England and Wales smoke-free by 2030.

Dominic Raab, the Justice Secretary, on Thursday said the Department of Health and Social Care is exploring ways to tackle youth vaping in response to a question in the Commons.

'Appalling' marketing of vapes

Last month, England's chief medical officer attacked the 'appalling' marketing of vapes to children – saying it was clear some products are intended to appeal to under-age people.

Professor Sir Chris Whitty told MPs: 'I think everyone agrees that marketing vaping, an addictive product, with, as you imply, unknown consequences for developing minds, to children is utterly unacceptable. Yet it is happening.

'There's no doubt it's happening because, although from a low base, the rates of vaping have doubled in the last couple of years among children. So that is an appalling situation.'

Experts said that children were being attracted to disposable e-cigarettes, in fruity flavours, being used by people on TikTok and Instagram.

While it is illegal to sell vapes to under-18s, social media carries posts from teenagers showing the new vapes and discussing the flavours, which include pink lemonade and mango.

Over the past year, a new generation of disposable vapes known as 'puff bars', which contain nicotine, have come on to the market.

During the select committee, Dr Caroline Johnson, Conservative MP for Sleaford and North Hykeham, said vapes were 'heavily marketed at children, which is developing into a whole generation of teenagers completely addicted to sucking little nicotine coloured pop things.'

The chief medical officer said e-cigarettes were a useful tool for adults trying to stop smoking.

Key Facts

- In 2013 3% of 11-15 year olds had vaped, this rose to 8% in 2022.

- 1% of teens in Spain regularly use e-cigarettes, compared to 7% of teens in Britain.

But he questioned whether there is any need at all for flavoured and fruity e-cigarettes, amid growing concern that such products appeal to children.

'Encouraging people to vape'

Sir Chris said far more must be done to prevent children vaping, adding: 'Is it reasonable to have, in any case, flavours and colours that are clearly aimed at essentially encouraging people to vape who may well not be vaping at all?

'I think we need to be much more serious, in my view, that trying everything we can to reduce vaping in children, as well as smoking in children, is really important whilst trying what we can do to make sure that vaping is available for those for whom that is the route out of smoking.'

He added: 'Disposable vapes – things like Elf Bar – are clearly the kinds of products which look as if they're being marketed, in reality, at children.

'And I think we should look very seriously at these products for which the child market appears to be the principal market and say "why are we considering this to be a good thing to have?".'

Last September, experts called for a crackdown on the sale of vapes to children and concluded little is known about the long-term impact of e-cigarettes on health.

The King's College London study, commissioned by the Office for Health Improvement and Disparities at the Department of Health, said it was clear that vaping is less harmful than cigarettes in the short to medium term and smokers should be encouraged to switch to vapes.

However, it said current research is not robust enough to make clear conclusions about how harmful vaping is in the longer term.

31 March 2023

Use of e-cigarettes among young people in Great Britain

Summary of key findings

The evolving youth use of e-cigarettes in Britain is monitored using the ASH Smokefree GB survey of 11-18 year olds 2013-2022 (see Appendix 2 for methodology), in the context of changes in tobacco use and the regulation of e-cigarettes (see Appendix 1). We present the results for 11-17 year olds separately from 18 year olds. It is an offence to sell e-cigarettes to children under 18 in the United Kingdom.

Use and awareness of e-cigarettes

- A large majority of 11-17 year olds have never tried or are unaware of e-cigarettes (83.8%).

- In 2022, 15.8% of 11-17 year olds had tried vaping, compared to 11.2% in 2021 and 13.9% in 2020.

- In 2022, 7.0% of 11-17 year olds were current users, compared to 3.3% in 2021 and 4.1% in 2020.

- Children under 16 are least likely to try e-cigarettes. 10.4% of 11-15 year olds have tried vaping, compared to 29.1% of 16-17 year olds. Among 18 year olds 40.8% report having tried an e-cigarette.

- Use among 11-17 year olds who have never smoked remains low and largely experimental, while 7.5% of never smokers have tried an e-cigarette in 2022 only 1.7% report at least monthly use.

Attitudes towards vaping

- Reasons for using e-cigarettes differ between children who smoke and those who haven't. While children who haven't smoked are significantly more likely to report their main reason for using one was 'just to give it a try' (65.4%) among those who smoke they are significantly more likely to report that they 'enjoy the experience' (17.5%) are 'trying to quit smoking' (10.7%) or are 'addicted to them' (10.3%).

- The misperception that e-cigarettes are more than or equally harmful as tobacco cigarettes rose from 2013 onwards and in 2022 was 40.9%, the same as in 2020. Only 42.1% of 11-17 year olds in 2022 believed that e-cigarettes were less harmful than cigarettes.

Main source and type of product used

- In 2022 for the first time the most frequently used product was a disposable vape (52.0% compared to 7.7% in 2021), with the most popular brands by far being Elf Bar and Geek Bar.

- The main source for both cigarettes and e-cigarettes is shops. 51.9% of 11-17 year olds get their cigarettes from shops and 46.5% get their e-cigarettes from shops.

In conclusion, use of e-cigarettes has increased in 2022 compared to 2021. However, use among never smokers remains low and mostly experimental. Likelihood of trying or currently using e-cigarettes increases with age and smoking status. The big increase in the use of disposable products has happened concurrently with higher levels of youth use, although the survey is cross sectional and so does not prove this is causal in either direction. Continued surveillance is needed.

July 2022

Wellness vapes: what you need to know about vaping vitamins and other supplements

An article from The Conversation.

By Aaron Scott, Associate Professor in Respiratory Science, University of Birmingham and Alice Jasper, Postdoctoral Research Fellow, Inflammation and Ageing, University of Birmingham

So-called wellness vapes are growing in popularity. Unlike regular vapes (e-cigarettes) that contain nicotine, these products contain vitamins, hormones or essential oils. But they have caught the attention of the US Food and Drug Administration (FDA) because of the unproven health claims made by many of the companies that sell them.

Wellness vapes – also known as 'nutritional supplement diffusers' – cover a range of products that find a common origin in e-cigarettes. E-cigarettes deliver nicotine to the lungs without the need for combustion or tobacco. This removes some harmful components, such as tobacco tar. Instead of combustion, e-cigarettes use energy from a battery to heat e-liquid, which forms a vapour that can be inhaled.

A new wave of products aims to use this same inhaled delivery system for a wide range of non-nicotine products, including vitamins (B12 and C are particularly popular), milk thistle, melatonin (a hormone), green tea and a variety of essential oils. Wellness vape companies make claims that different combinations of these additives can help you focus better, promote sleep and even help you lose weight.

Inhaling rather than swallowing these compounds results in faster absorption into the bloodstream, so, theoretically, the vitamins and supplements could act faster when inhaled.

Many of these additives will be individually familiar as supplements that are rated as safe for ingestion. But the vast majority lack inhalation safety testing, particularly of potential long-term harms. Because wellness vapes don't contain nicotine, they evade the regulators.

The incidence of e-cigarette-related acute lung injury (Evali) in the US in 2019 highlights the importance of testing the route of intake. In the 60 deaths from Evali initially reported, vitamin E acetate was identified as a key agent that caused lung damage in these people. Vitamin E is a common food additive, so this clearly highlights how even well-known substances can have very serious health consequences when inhaled.

These devices are quite new to the market, so there is little research on their safety. However, we can consider the specific components to look for potential effects, whether beneficial or harmful.

E-liquid components

Many benign or beneficial compounds can become harmful if given in an untested way or given to the wrong patient group. For example, the benefits of vitamin C are universally known, yet the use of high-dose vitamin C has been shown to increase the risk of death in people with sepsis.

Vitamin B12 is also a popular additive for these devices. In people who are deficient in the vitamin, a B12 injection is very effective in restoring levels. Yet there is a distinct lack of supporting evidence for any benefits to people with normal B12 levels. Also, we lack evidence on the safety or effectiveness of inhaled B12.

One study carried out in 1967 showed no benefit to inhaling vitamin B12 over supplementation by injection. But even in 1967, the researchers were careful to point out the potential for lung damage.

We can also look at information from shared components with e-cigarettes to look for potential effects. Some products deliver vitamin B12 dissolved in a common e-liquid component, vegetable glycerine. Other products use propylene glycol or a mixture of both liquids. When heated, these components break down into harmful chemicals, termed reactive carbonyl species, such as formaldehyde.

These chemicals have been shown to harm alveolar macrophages, important immune cells in the lung, in a way not dependent on the presence of nicotine. Similar findings have also been shown in other important airway and immune cells.

Wellness vapes delivering essential oils may also suffer from the same concerns. They contain compounds called terpenes and a mixture of other chemicals similar to e-liquids.

Terpenes have been reported to have a range of benefits including anticancer, antiallergy and antimicrobial properties, suggesting the potential benefits of taking these essential oils. However, terpenes are degraded by heat so may be broken down by vaping into harmful compounds that can irritate the airways and may be toxic to cells at higher doses and longer exposure.

Increased scrutiny

Given the similarities between e-cigarettes and wellness vapes, these companies are now facing increased scrutiny from public health bodies. The FDA has warned that wellness vapes are 'unsafe', 'ineffective' and 'unproven'.

We must carefully weigh the benefits and risks of use. Many of the supplements in these devices may help improve our lifestyles, but there is no evidence to support the benefits of inhalation over traditional methods of delivery.

While wellness vapes have not been around long enough for researchers to know for certain the long-term consequences of their use. We know that short-term exposure to their components can harm the lungs, so prolonged use may pose a very serious risk – one that tips the scales of evidence firmly against the use of 'wellness vapes'.

16 August 2022

THE CONVERSATION

What is behind Gen Z's Elf Bar obsession?

Despite e-cigarettes being deeply uncool just a few years ago, young people are flocking to the brightly coloured disposable vapes known as Elf Bars. Ellie Muir got lost in a puff of flavoured smoke to investigate how we got here.

By Ellie Muir

Enter a UK nightclub tonight and you will find yourself surrounded by an inescapable cloud of fruity smoke. This candied plume of vapour comes from an Elf Bar, Gen Z's newest accessory. The Elf Bar is a new, pre-filled disposable vape device that's slimmer and more compact than a normal e-cigarette. In windows of discount phone shops and off licences and sold inside nightclubs and supermarkets, the hot pink, neon yellow and red-berry pens are neatly lined up in colour order like a fresh packet of Crayolas. They're clutched in the hands of teenagers right the way through to young professionals, pulled out of bum bags at raves or perched on the table at after-work drinks.

On TikTok, young people are selling DIY Elf Bar holders, or reviewing each of the brand's 28 flavours as though they're critiquing a meal at a Michelin-star restaurant. One user (@ ishaq_jpeg) even makes cocktail recipes inspired by the most popular Elf Bar flavours. The popularity of disposable vapes has soared in the last 12 months, according to Dan Judd, head of digital for Vape Superstore, one of the leading online vape suppliers in the UK. 'Elf Bar sales have grown exponentially, with around a 450 per cent increase in the last six months,' he says. 'We have also seen a new type of customer who is only buying disposable devices.'

Elf Bars are manufactured in China, the base of their headquarters, and first launched in 2018. Classic flavours include 'blue razz lemonade', 'kiwi passionfruit guava' and 'blueberry sour raspberry' – all of which have been turned

into TikTok cocktails. The most popular pen, the Elf Bar 600, is disposable and comes pre-filled with 20mg of nicotine salt liquid infused into the flavoured e-liquid. They last for around 600 puffs per bar, with prices starting as low as £4.95 on Vape Superstore, or five bars for £20. In comparison, a 20-pack of Benson and Hedges is more than double the price and arrives with 24mg of nicotine per pack. Both contain a similar amount of nicotine – it just depends on how quickly a smoker can get through them.

Until the Elf Bar appeared on the UK market, vaping was most associated among young people with Ethan Bradberry, a character from the viral comedy sketch video Vape Nation. In the clip, first posted on YouTube in 2016, comedian Ethan Klein walks around New York City parodying vapers. From here, the archetype of the 'vape bro' was rapidly turned into a meme, vaping becoming a universally recognised code for the ridiculously uncool. When the meme trended in 2016, anyone who held an e-cigarette between their fingers or blew a vape ring would be scoffed at – much in the same way that 'Crypto Bros' are currently recoiled at in 2022. Now, though, Elf Bar users shamelessly flood nightclub smoking areas and proudly announce their favourite flavours to strangers. It's almost as if vaping has been shed of its 'vape bro' connotations, taken on by a generation adopting the snazzier, sleeker bars.

'Part of the allure of disposable Elf Bar products is a combination of the wide availability, the cheapness and portability of the product, and the fact that it's easily shareable,' says Hazel Cheeseman, deputy chief executive of Action on Smoking Health (ASH).

The allure is attracting even non-smokers. Ali, a 22-year-old King's College London dentistry student, says he never flirted with the idea of smoking cigarettes but found himself drawn to Elf Bars last year when he first started seeing them in shops. 'There are just loads of colours and you get excited with all the different flavours,' he says over the phone, his Elf Bar crackling down the line as he takes a deep inhale in between sentences. 'It's a pastime. I roll over in bed and my Elf Bar is there. It's just convenient.'

Ali says that he and his friends try new flavours together, and even different disposable brands like Elux. 'I never used to see that many people with Elf Bars, but now I'll leave the house where I live in north London and see everyone using them,' he says. For Nirvana Henry, 21, who works at a Soho House members club, it's the convenience of being able to vape indoors or at a nightclub that won her over. And not having to smell of cigarette smoke afterwards. 'I vape when I'm getting ready for my day, walking to work, or at the pub or club.' Maybe the allure is just that simple – Elf Bars slot neatly into the lives of young people. Plus they taste good.

In 2003, electronic cigarettes were developed in Beijing by pharmacist and inventor Hon Lik as an alternative to conventional smoking, and emerged on the UK market in 2007. Cheeseman says that the products have fulfilled their intended purpose. 'Vapes have helped thousands of people stop smoking,' she says. 'Vaping is substantially less harmful than smoking and electronic cigarettes have a very important public health role to play.'

Gillian Golden, CEO of the Independent British Vape Trade Association (IBVTA), concurs with this view. 'Disposable vapes have enabled a very large number of adult smokers to break the habit of smoking. We've seen that over the last 18 months, and it's one of the reasons we've seen one of the lowest smoking rates ever in this country.' But Golden remains sceptical about the disposable nature of the Elf Bar and similar single-use products – like the Elf Bar's clunkier sibling, the Geek Bar. 'There are cheaper ways to vape with a rechargeable and refillable device that's better for the planet,' she says. Those are products like the Innokin EQ FLTR that come with 100 per cent biodegradable filter tips, or e-cigarette products with longer battery life, like the Aspire Pockex.

Vaping, though, is as un-chic as it was when Ethan Bradberry paraded around New York City – it's just that Gen Z-ers are happily embracing the tackiness (and the flaws) of the devices. Vapes fail to replicate the elegance of smoking a cigarette. Remember Scarlett Johansson effortlessly lighting up in Match Point, and perching the vessel on her pursed lips? You won't get that here. With their brightly coloured, highlighter pen aesthetic, Elf Bars just don't conjure the same suave. Gen Z vapers know it. They're aware that smoking something that resembles a stationery item is wildly inelegant. They're aware that it's excessive to buy multiple Bars each week. They're aware that the Elf Bar's long-term effects are still hazy. They adopt it proudly, though, even if slightly ironically.

The EU is currently trying to place a ban on flavoured vapes, while the 18+ devices are finding their way into the hands of children. But Gen Z's nihilistic embrace of Elf Bars has transformed vaping from one of the most heavily derided ways to pass time into an essential accessory. Even non-smokers are joining in. But behind the popularity of the pens, vapers are slowly beginning to question their fixation. Ali, along with his group of friends who similarly love Elf Bars, have all been trying to break away from the habit, but keep getting lured back by new flavours. 'The scary thing about Elf Bars is because it's a new craze, we don't even know about the long-term effects,' he says, inquisitively.

Though it's not entirely clear whether Ali's trying to convince me or himself, he sounds determined to ditch the disposable vape and shift his lifestyle. 'I know that I can and will quit when I want to.'

21 August 2022

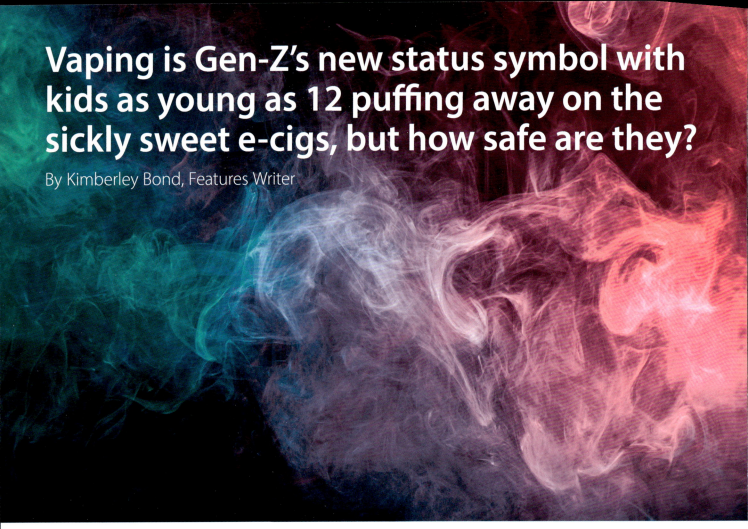

Vaping is Gen-Z's new status symbol with kids as young as 12 puffing away on the sickly sweet e-cigs, but how safe are they?

By Kimberley Bond, Features Writer

Julie Fields* had a hunch one day last year that her 14-year-old son Ben* was doing something he shouldn't be. Nothing particularly prompted her into thinking this – call it a mother's intuition, if you will.

When he was out with friends one day, the 44-year-old checked Ben's bedside drawer and saw two vapes tucked away.

Julie didn't hit the roof at what she found. Instead, she removed the offending e-cigarettes – or 'bars' as they're also known – and decided to wait until Ben noticed.

It took a few months until he did, and the two had a frank conversation about his newly acquired habit.

'He said he'd been smoking them for a year, and had got them off a friend from school,' Julie, who lives just outside Bristol, explains to Metro.co.uk. 'He said he'd only vape when stressed, and at sleepovers, but not doing it all the time, every day.'

While she was grateful for his honesty, Julie was taken aback that Ben had gotten into vaping so young, particularly as he's a fitness-conscious youngster who plays rugby and football.

'Ben hates smoking, he hates being around people that smoke, so I was surprised he was vaping,' she admits. 'But I don't think he sees it in quite the same way. I think he sees it in the same way as eating sweets.'

Ben himself isn't concerned, shrugging off any suggestion vaping could be bad for him.

'I prefer vaping over cigarettes because cigarettes have a significant impact on your health and vapes have a combination of flavours and look better,' he tells us.

'I'm not worried about it affecting my performance in sports because after vaping for a while, I noticed no difference at all.'

However, Julie herself is less thrilled at the prospect of her underage son puffing away on e-cigarettes.

'I'd rather he didn't do it. Like I'd rather he didn't drink alcohol,' she says. 'But he is 14. For the main part, each teenager is trying to find out where they fit. If their peers are doing it, and they don't, how does that look?'

Ben is one of many in the UK who are eschewing 'real' cigarettes for the electronic kind, a habit which has rapidly grown popular in recent years; the UK vaping market is now worth more than £1 billion alone.

A recent survey by Action on Smoking and Health found that in England, around four million people vape regularly, compared to six million who smoke.

However, it's the younger end of the population that are swapping cigs for bars: vaping in people aged 11-18 had doubled from 4% in 2020 to 8.6% in 2022.

Traditional cigarette smoking figures for the same age-group had gone down slightly from 6.7% in 2020 to 6.0% in 2022.

With soaring numbers of young people taking up the habit, the Department of Health and Social Care commissioned the Institute of Psychiatry, Psychology and Neuroscience team from King's College London to undertake the biggest review of its kind on vaping and its comparison to cigarettes.

The study found that while smoking cigarettes is worse for your health than vaping, choosing to vape is not entirely free from risk. Many still contain nicotine, a highly addictive chemical that can increase in blood pressure, heart rate, flow of blood to the heart and a narrowing of the arteries – and a new study has shown e-cigarettes were found to cause similar damage to blood vessels as smoking tobacco.

A recent investigation found that a popular brand of vapes were at least 50 per cent over the legal limit for nicotine e-liquid. As a response, some major retailers have pulled the vapes from the shelves.

However, Ben has no complaints after vaping fairly regularly for a year – well, bar a few.

'I've noticed no adverse effects since I started vaping, apart from an occasional dry mouth, known as "cotton mouth," he says. 'And if you do too much vaping in a short period of time you get a stomach, also known as "nic sick" or a "nic rush" where you get dizzy – but in a good way.'

However, Chad Texiera's excessive vaping throughout 2020 saw him question whether his penchant for e-cigarettes was actually doing him damage.

The 26-year-old, who had smoked occasionally for four years beforehand, decided to switch to vapes two years ago. With the small plastic device never far from his reach, he'd disappear behind a plume of synthetic strawberry flavoured smoke – far more regularly compared to when he was smoking actual cigarettes.

'I'd only ever really smoke socially before, on nights out with friends, or whenever I was stressed,' Chad explains. 'I'd been a smoker for four years before I moved on to vapes, because I really dislike the smell of cigarettes, it's f***ing disgusting. Vaping was easier – there's no smell and you can do it indoors.

'I used to smoke when I was stressed, but with vapes, I found I was just doing it out of boredom. When I was working on a laptop, when I was watching TV, cooking, whatever... I was basically vaping for the fun of it.'

At the peak of his habit in 2020, Chad, who works as a CEO for a comms and marketing company, found himself going through at least one vape a day – roughly the equivalent nicotine of between 48 – 50 cigarettes. And at £5 a pop, he was easily spending around £200 to fund his habit.

However, around the same time, Chad found himself getting increasingly ill – shortness of breath, sleepiness, headaches and a constant dry cough, accompanied by a sore throat. Initially, he thought he'd succumbed to Covid – but when Chad started having heart palpitations and suffered from bleeding gums, he realised it might be something else.

'I saw my dentist and she put all these problems down to vaping,' he says. 'In conjunction with all my other symptoms, I was like: "Oh God, this is killing me!" I knew I really had to stop.'

Dr Alka Patel believes that far more needs to be done for people to be made aware of the risks of trying vapes which contain a substance as highly as addictive as nicotine.

'Comparing vapes to cigarettes is like comparing mercury to arsenic – both dangerous in their own way, and neither safe,' she tells Metro.co.uk. 'I suspect the serious dangers of vapes will emerge over the next decade but we have to learn from history and not allow alternatives to cigarettes which continue to expose us to harmful chemicals to be an acceptable alternative.

'We're creating a next level generation of addiction – it's a public health catastrophe where control is given away to manufacturers and advertising giants.'

Dr Patel continues: 'We know that heating the metal coils in vapes results in toxic metals appearing in lung and blood fluids. A meta-analysis in 2020 showed aluminum, antimony, arsenic, cadmium, cobalt, chromium, copper, iron, lead, manganese, nickel, selenium, tin, and zinc in vapes and e-cigarettes. I have concerns about how vaping is marketed as more healthy when we are nowhere close enough to be able to say that.

'What we can say with confidence however is that vapers are inhaling a mix of thousands of complex chemicals and we have no idea what they are or what they are doing. Now what we need to do is to connect the dots between these metals and cognitive dysfunction, kidney damage, immune impairment, abdominal pain, tiredness and more. We're letting public hunger run ahead before we've learnt how to walk with the science first.'

Despite this lack of knowledge or even awareness of the risks that vaping could pose, it hasn't stopped young people being intrigued by this relatively new phenomenon.

Gone are the days of sneaking behind the bike shed to try your first illicit Marlboro Light, with teachers now reporting a rise in vaping amongst secondary school pupils.

Blackpool Conservative councillor Andrew Stansfield recently claimed vaping was 'rife' in the town's schools, and estimated that 75% of students were using e-cigarettes.

One London-based teacher, who requested not to be named, said he was asked to break up an illicit 'vape club' that took place once a week in the girls' toilets, where girls as young as 11 were bringing in different flavoured vapes to try. Another parent was left baffled when her pre-teen daughter asked if she could buy a vape for her friend, also 12, for Christmas.

It's something Lucy Baker, 46, has been particularly aware of in more recent weeks herself, as she's observed her 12-year-old daughter becoming more intrigued with vaping.

'She's hugely curious about vapes,' Lucy tells Metro.co.uk. 'She tells me the majority of her friends have tried it or are all vaping – and that's just in Year 7.

'She said that she went to her friend's house after school one day, and the 11-year-old daughter and her mum were sharing a vape.

'If I take my eldest to school or shopping in our nearest town of Lincoln, I see people of all ages puffing away on vapes. You don't even need to go to a specialist shop to buy them anymore – there's shelves and shelves of them in the newsagents.'

Lucy, who works as a confidence coach, agrees that vaping is effectively regarded by children in a similar way to how Gen X'ers may have seen smoking in their youth, and may be feeling peer pressure to join in.

'I try and warn her that vapes contain nicotine, which is addictive,' she says. 'But she says it won't happen to her, she won't get hooked. We've all said that at some point in our lives, and it's only when you come an adult and look back, you realise, actually, those cigarettes were addictive.

'We're having quite an open conversation about it, but it's quite a fraught one as I'm obviously telling her not to be so ridiculous.'

Lucy also fears the lack of knowledge available to children and parents alike means that no-one is wholly aware of the risks of vaping.

'I don't think there's an awareness of kids at all that vapes are effectively more than just sweets,' she says. 'Unlike cigarettes, vaping devices can come in pretty pastel colours and be covered in glitter. They don't taste gross like cigarettes, they can be fruity and sweet, so it doesn't feel like they're bad for you.

'Vaping is definitely the status symbol of the younger generation. My daughter is adamant everyone around her is doing it. I know for a fact she's taken my husband's vape before and has recorded herself on her phone, vaping.'

Lucy believes it's the influence of social media brands, such as TikTok, which are partly responsible in seeing so many young people become vape-curious.

'TikTok makes me so angry because I can't police what she sees on there,' Lucy says. 'So much on there is not verified or fact checked. She just sees lots of people vaping and thinks she should be too.'

TikTok in particular has been criticised for helping fuel the boom in e-cigarettes, after a broadsheet investigation found that some brands were paying influencers to promote their vapes in videos.

It's a clear violation of the Advertising Standards Agency, which explicitly forbids ads for nicotine-containing e-cigarettes not licensed as medicines across every media platform.

And with TikTok being the app of choice for young people, with half of eight to 11-year-olds and three-quarters of 16 to 17-year-olds using the app regularly, the platform has been criticised by public health charities for not doing enough to sanction those who violate advertising standards.

Deborah Arnott, chief executive of Action on Smoking and Health (ASH), explained to Metro.co.uk: 'Vaping is not risk free. Although the evidence is clear that it's much less harmful than smoking and can help smokers quit, if you don't smoke, don't vape. The glamorous promotion of vaping to young people on social media is completely inappropriate and TikTok is one of the worst offenders, they need to take responsibility and turn off the tap.'

In response, a spokesperson from TikTok told Metro.co.uk: 'At TikTok, keeping our community safe is a top priority. We prohibit content that depicts or promotes the sale, trade or offer of tobacco, including vaping products, and we will remove any content found to violate our Community Guidelines. We also do not recommend content that shows or promotes tobacco products in TikTok users' feeds.'

The UK Vaping Industry Association (UKVIA) are also stepping up to ensure those who are underage cannot purchase vapes.

'The UKVIA takes the issue of youth vaping extremely seriously,' John Dunne, Director General of the UK Vaping Industry Association, told Metro.co.uk. 'Our code of practice already has a significant emphasis on safeguarding against vape products getting into the hands of minors. When joining the association, members have to commit to never selling vaping products to anyone under 18 years old and apply a "Challenge 25" policy in all retail environments.

'We are doing everything possible to cut off the sales of vapes to Under 18 year olds at source, working closely with Trading Standards and retail trade bodies across the country.'

Dunne continued: 'More recently we wrote to the Secretary of State for Health and Social Care and proposed a number of recommendations to come down hard on those who sell vapes to minors. This included the introduction of a retail licensing or approved retailer and distributor scheme; increased penalties of at least £10,000 per instance for

traders who flout UK law; and the introduction of a national test purchasing scheme to ensure all the country's retail operations are performing to high standards when it comes to preventing youth access to e-cigarettes.'

However, for Lucy, these actions are too little, too late, when so many youngsters already have access to e-cigarettes.

'I know it sounds drastic, but I think vapes need to be totally banned,' she says. 'I don't think any amount of parents or schools saying "don't do it" will make a difference.

'They're too attractive, they look fun, they taste fun, they're all about fun, but underlying is possible addiction and spending all your money on a vape.

'People forget that these aren't adults who have all the information to make an informed choice as to whether to vape or not. These are kids. I don't want my children to get addicted to nicotine. I don't want to deal with my kid who wants to spend her pocket money on a vape because she's addicted.'

The damage done by excessive nicotine consumption can be undone, says Dr Patel – but only if 'it's stopped early'.

'The longer you vape the more inflammation becomes ingrained in your lungs, resulting in chronic changes at a cellular level, the more the metal toxicity takes effect at a cellular level and the more the DNA damage becomes irreversible.

'Don't be fooled into thinking that vaping is a healthy alternative to smoking cigarettes just because you want it to be.'

For Julie, she knows she can't prevent Ben vaping, unless she physically bans him from leaving the house.

However, she does worry that vaping may lead to a 'gateway' for more harmful habits.

'The bottom line is, I can't stop him from doing it,' she admits. 'If I had magic words of wisdom that would have an effect, I would use them. And we just don't know if vaping does lead to longer-term damage. To be honest, if I was presenting him with studies saying vapes caused serious diseases, I still don't think it'll stop him – teenagers think they're invincible and that it won't happen to them.'

She continues: 'I'd rather he was vaping than smoking or trying spliffs, but I don't know where he is, or what he would or wouldn't do. I'm hoping it's a passing fad, and that he grows out of it.'

Ben, however, has other ideas.

'I think I'm addicted, sometimes I'm at home and think I'd really like a nic rush, or I wish I had a vape on me,' he says. 'I can potentially see myself vaping in the near [future] and further.

'I'm not worried about potential side effects which might occur in the long run, though.'

Names have been changed

6 February 2023

School children favour vaping over smoking or taking drugs

Fewer school children are smoking or taking drugs, but vaping use among 11 to 15-year-olds is increasing, a study from NHS Digital finds.

In 2021, 9% of school children aged 11 to 15 years old report vaping on a regular or occasional basis. This comes at an increase of 6% since 2018.

Which children are vaping?

The report found that 1 in 5 UK 15-year-old girls vape and 18% of all 15-year-olds are current e-cigarette users.

Statistics revealed that 23% of children who met people outside of school or the home every day were vaping, compared to 1% of those who didn't venture out socially.

In the UK, the number of people considered regular smokers and e-cigarette users more than doubled, from 29% of regular smokers in 2018 to 61% in 2021.

'I wake up with a tight chest every morning'

Priscilla, a source for Open Access Government, explained that she first started vaping at 15 years old and like many other children, has been addicted ever since. Now at 21 years old, she comments on her symptoms:

'I can feel it on my chest and I wake up with a tight chest every morning. Previously, I only used my inhaler for my allergies but now I need to use it every day.

'I regret starting vaping at school. I know I need to quit but it's hard.'

Only 3% of British school children smoke cigarettes

The Smoking, Drinking and Drug Use among Young People in England, 2021 report found that cigarette use has decreased by 5% since 2018.

'The lowest level ever recorded'

In 2021, only 3% of students smoked. In addition, only 12% reported having ever smoked, a decrease from 16% in 2018, and the lowest level ever recorded.

The report focuses on smoking, drinking and drug use and contains results from a biennial survey of secondary school pupils in England years 7-11 (mostly aged 11-15).

In 2021, 18% of school children had taken drugs

According to this survey, fewer young people are taking drugs. 18% of pupils reported having ever taken drugs, a decline from 24% in 2018 and in the last year, 12% of pupils said they had taken drugs, down from 17% in 2018.

'Cannabis is the most popular drug amongst school children'

6% of children said they had taken cannabis in 2021, down from 8% in 2018.

In terms of class A drugs, use amongst children has remained at around 2-3% since 2010.

Of those who reported taking drugs on more than one occasion, 19% said they took drugs alone on the most recent occasion, up from 11% in 2018, and 7% in 2016.

Alcohol use has not changed since 2018

6% of pupils aged 11 to 15 years old said they usually drank alcohol at least once a week. This figure has not changed since 2018.

Among those who reported drinking, 6% said they usually drank alone, an increase from 3% in 2018.

How did Covid-19 impact smoking, drinking and drug use?

Undoubtedly the pandemic impacted the way children interacted with substances. NHS Digital analysed pupils school learning and socialising in the last school year (September 2020 to July 2021).

Researchers found that school children who regularly met up with people outside their school or home were more likely to have recently smoked, drank alcohol or taken drugs.

Of pupils who met with people outside of school every day, the results were the following:

- 9% were current smokers
- 12% usually drank alcohol once a week
- 19% had taken drugs in the last month

Results differed drastically for those individuals who had not met people outside of school in the past four weeks. For those school children, these proportions fell to 1%, 2%, and 2% respectively.

Low levels of life satisfaction for 57% of schoolchildren who use substances

NHS Digital also wanted to study the well-being of schoolchildren, and how this may be linked to smoking, alcohol and drug use.

Pupils were asked questions about life satisfaction, happiness, and anxiety.

Low levels of life satisfaction were experienced by 57% of young people who had recently smoked, drank alcohol and taken drugs. This compared to 35% who had recently done just one of these things, and 18% who had not recently smoked, drank or taken drugs.

15 September 2022

Why do opponents of vaping want to suppress or dismiss science?

We need to learn more, not less, about e-cigarettes.

By Marc Gunther

E-cigarettes have fractured the tobacco-control community. Some researchers argue that vaping nicotine saves lives by helping smokers quit. Others say that e-cigarettes are dangerous, especially for young people. The debate is by no means settled.

So you'd think that all involved would welcome more science. Sadly, that's not so.

Consider, for example, what happened after a debate about conflicts of interest in tobacco science, part of a seminar series organized by academics.

One one side: Joanna Cohen, the Bloomberg Professor of Disease Prevention at the Bloomberg School of Public Health at Johns Hopkins University. She argued that journals such as Tobacco Control, where she is an editor, are right in refusing to publish research sponsored by the industry. What's more, she said, those who work in the industry, including at e-cigarette company Juul, should be prohibited from attending scientific conferences.

'Scientists do not want their journals or their scientific societies to be used in the service of an industry that continues to perpetuate the most deadly disease epidemic of our time,' Cohen said.

On the other side: Kenneth Michael Cummings, a professor at the Medical University of South Carolina. Cummings, a veteran of the tobacco wars who has testified in court against cigarette companies, nevertheless does not believe that they should be barred from journals or scientific meetings.

'Science ought to be judged on its merits. Period,' Cummings said. 'Censorship is not the way to go.' Companies that make reduced-risk products like e-cigarettes could be part of the solution to the public health threat posed by combustible tobacco, he said.

Watching online, I thought Cummings got the better of the debate. Cohen, evidently, felt the same way – because a week or so later, she sent an email to Matthew Myers, the president of the Campaign for Tobacco-Free Kids, an ardent opponent of all things tobacco, including e-cigarettes:

Good morning Matt. I hope you and your family are well.

I'm looking for an expert who can help me effectively respond to arguments about not allowing tobacco company research in journals, and not allowing tobacco company employees to attend scientific conferences. Those in favour of tobacco company publishing/conference attendance are calling the above policies 'censorship' and they talk about 'open science' (quite powerful on the face of it).

I thought you may be aware of people/companies who are very good at crafting message framing that resonates well (and who don't work for tobacco companies!). Or, if you can recommend who I might ask, that would be greatly appreciated too!

All the best,

Joanna

Do you see the problem here?

'The aim of suppressing science'

The professor who opposes conflicts of interest turns for help – specifically, help finding a PR consultant – to an advocate who is leading the war against vaping. Perhaps coincidentally, Cohen, Johns Hopkins and Tobacco-Free Kids all get funding from Michael Bloomberg and his foundation, Bloomberg Philanthropies, which gave Tobacco-Free Kids a three-year, $160 million grant to oppose vaping in 2019. Bloomberg and the foundation have donated more than $3 billion to Hopkins, which named its public health school after him.

Clive Bates, a British advocate for reduced-harm nicotine products, including e-cigarettes, said the email exchange 'illustrates an interesting collaborative operation between a venerable academic institution and an activist operation, both Bloomberg funded, with the aim of suppressing science from sources they do not like.'

The collaboration is interesting, but is it objectionable? Perhaps not. Both camps in the contentious debate about vaping coordinate efforts behind the scenes. Cohen, a respected tobacco researcher, is not known as a hard-line opponent of vaping. 'The research (about vaping) is limited and it's a moving target,' she told me, when we spoke back earlier this year. She declined to talk with me about her email.

What is objectionable is that Cohen and Tobacco-Free Kids want to reject or discredit science that could shed light on the debate about how to regulate e-cigarettes.

To be sure, tobacco companies have a disgraceful record of distorting science, lying to the public and marketing to kids. They continue to sell vast quantities of deadly cigarettes – about $700 billion worth this year. One in five adults in the world smokes tobacco, according to Our World in Data.

On the other hand, the good news – for public health, if not for the industry – is that smoking rates are falling almost everywhere. Some of that decline surely is due to the rise of vaping. So tobacco companies, including Altria, which is the biggest shareholder in Juul, R.J. Reynolds and British American Tobacco, are investing in e-cigarettes for sound business reasons: They see alternative nicotine-delivery products as a way to offset the declines in their revenues and profits from combustible tobacco. Strange as it seems, their interests may be aligned with those who care about public health.

Industry research should be read sceptically, of course, but it can help researchers and regulators understand how to move smokers off combustibles and onto less harmful products – a goal embraced by the FDA. One peer-reviewed study from Juul, for example, found that more than half of 17,000 cigarette smokers who bought a Juul starter kit had stopped smoking a year later and switched to vapes.

Instead of responding to that finding with curiosity, Matt Myers of Tobacco-Free Kids dismissed it, saying that 'research funded by tobacco companies cannot be treated as a credible source of science of evidence' because of the industry's history of lying. But the Juul study was submitted to the FDA as part of its application to remain on the market; getting caught misleading regulators could mean the end of Juul.

Meanwhile, Myers says nothing, at least in public, when shoddy science is deployed to support the anti-vaping cause. To the contrary – the longtime anti-tobacco crusader Stanton Glantz remained a go-to scientist for Tobacco-Free Kids and Parents Against Vaping E-Cigarettes (PAVE) even after some of his research into vaping was retracted and refuted. The journal *Tobacco Control*, where Joanna Cohen is an editor, continues to publish work by Glantz of highly questionable value.

Unintended consequences

More broadly, Tobacco-Free Kids and PAVE have taken the their crusade against e-cigarettes into the political arena rather than leave regulation to the FDA. Tobacco-Free Kids lobbies for state and local bans on flavoured e-cigarettes, like one recently passed in Washington, D.C. (Deadly cigarettes remain on the market.) PAVE is running a campaign called Back to School, Not Back to Juul, urging parents to demand that the FDA ban all flavoured cigarettes. Neither Tobacco-Free Kids nor PAVE – which was started and funded by well-to-do parents in Manhattan and Silicon Valley alarmed by youth vaping – display any interest in the fate of adult smokers, or in the millions of former adult smokers who have kicked the habit with the help of flavoured vapes. For the new prohibitionists, it's always about the kids and only about the kids.

Nor do they seem perturbed by the growing evidence that policies that ban vaping or impose steeper taxes on e-cigarettes lead more people to smoke.

'Unfortunately, we're seeing some recent data suggesting that where there have been severe restrictions placed on e-cigarettes, flavour bans and that sort of thing, smoking rates are going back up,' says Raymond Niaura, a professor at the NYU public health school who specializes in tobacco issues. 'Is this what the tobacco control community wants?'

For the moment, the future of e-cigarettes rests with the FDA and its Center for Tobacco Products, which is led by Mitch Zeller, a respected veteran of the tobacco wars. The regulators have been tasked with trying to settle the thorny question of whether e-cigarettes are 'appropriate for the protection of public health.' More than 500 staff members have spent years studying the issue, weighing the risks of e-cigs to young people against their benefits to adult smokers. The agency is expected to decide next month whether e-cigarettes can remain on the market.

Soon enough, we'll see how the new prohibitionists respond.

Disclosure: Readers have asked if I have sought or accepted money or other benefits from tobacco or e-cigarette companies. I have not and will not. Like many scientists who study vaping, I come to the topic with a point of view but try to remain open to new evidence. I'm writing about tobacco policy because I think it's important and deserves more attention.

18 August 2021

The regulation of e-cigarettes

This briefing paper provides an overview on the regulation of e-cigarettes.

By Elizabeth Rough

The new European Union Tobacco Products Directive (TPD) entered into force on 19 May 2014. It introduced new regulatory controls on electronic cigarettes (e-cigarettes), as well as setting out requirements on tobacco products. The UK Tobacco and Related Products Regulations 2016 implemented the TPD in full. This Commons Library Briefing Paper outlines the new product requirements for e-cigarettes and identifies where national regulations have gone beyond what is in the TPD.

The use of e-cigarettes

Unlike conventional cigarettes, e-cigarettes do not contain tobacco, do not involve burning and thus do not produce carbon monoxide, tar or smoke. They work by heating a solution of water, flavouring, propylene glycol, and, typically, nicotine to create a vapour that the user inhales. Using an e-cigarette is often described as 'vaping' rather than smoking. It was estimated in 2019 that almost 3 million people (5.7%) aged 18 and over in Great Britain were using e-cigarettes, up from 3.7% of over 18s in 2014. Survey data indicates that consumers are increasingly turning to e-cigarettes as a means to cut back on smoking tobacco, or to quit tobacco completely.

Debates on the benefits and risks of e-cigarettes, particularly regarding their safety and health implications, are ongoing

and will continue as more evidence gradually becomes available. A review of the evidence to date, commissioned by Public Health England, reported in 2015 that 'best estimates show that e-cigarettes are 95% less harmful to your health than normal cigarettes' and that there was no current evidence to show that they were renormalising smoking, or increasing the uptake of tobacco cigarettes.

Regulation of e-cigarettes

Different approaches to regulating e-cigarettes have been adopted internationally. Prior to the introduction of the Tobacco Products Directive (TPD), the UK initially regulated e-cigarettes as consumer products that were subject to existing product safety regulations. Some countries went further and banned the sale, distribution and importation of e-cigarettes, while others have no regulations in place. An alternative approach, considered by the UK Government, was to regulate all nicotine-containing e-cigarettes as

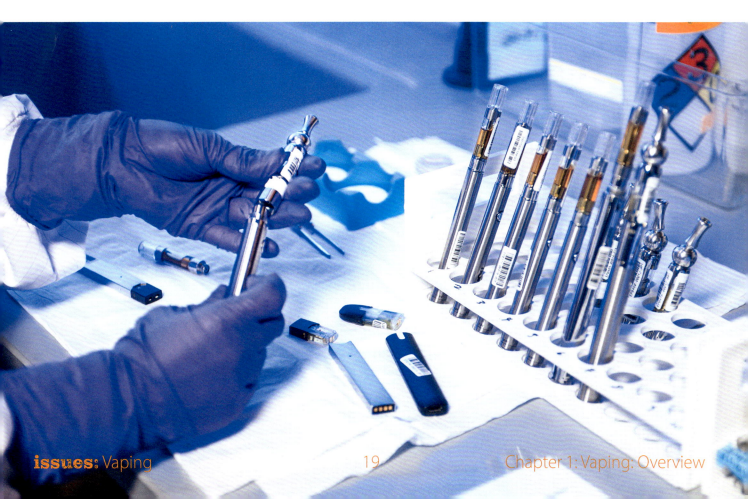

medicines. While the UK Medicines and Healthcare products Regulatory Agency set out plans in 2013 to implement this approach, they were superseded by the introduction of the TPD.

Tobacco Products Directive

The European Union Tobacco Products Directive entered into force on 19 May 2014, with the UK Tobacco and Related Products Regulations 2016 implementing the TPD in full across the UK. According to the European Commission, the TPD's aim is to 'improve the functioning of the internal market for tobacco and related products while ensuring a high level of health protection for European citizens'. Article 20 of the TPD introduces new regulatory controls for nicotine-containing e-cigarettes and refill containers, though it does not cover nicotine-containing products that are authorised as medicines. These controls aim to ensure:

- minimum standards for the safety and quality of all e-cigarettes and refill containers;

- that information is provided to consumers so that they can make informed choices;

- an environment that protects children from starting to use these products.

National regulations

The TPD does not seek to harmonise rules on:

- smoke-free environments;

- domestic advertising;

- domestic sales;

- age restrictions;

- nicotine–free cigarettes;

- flavourings of e-cigarettes.

These elements can all be regulated at a domestic level. England, Northern Ireland, Scotland and Wales have each introduced age restrictions on e-cigarettes that prohibit their sale to, and their purchase on behalf of, under 18s. In 2015/16 the Welsh Government attempted to go further and introduce controls on the use of e-cigarettes in public places, though the Bill was subsequently rejected by the Welsh Assembly. The Scottish Government has made provision, through the Health (Tobacco, Nicotine etc. and Care) (Scotland) Act 2016, to restrict the advertising of vapour products through secondary legislation, though this is not yet in place.

The Tobacco and Related Products Regulations 2016 were subsequently amended by the Tobacco Products and Nicotine Inhaling Products (Amendment Etc.) (EU Exit) Regulations 2019 and 2020 to enable tobacco and e-cigarette regulation to continue to function following the UK's withdrawal from the EU.

The Department of Health and Social Care has a statutory duty to review the regulatory impact of the Tobacco and Related Products Regulations 2016 by May 2021 and publish a report setting out the conclusions of the review. At the time of writing the results of the review had not been published.

Select Committee Inquiry

On 25 October 2017, the House of Commons Science and Technology Select Committee launched an Inquiry to look at the science behind e-cigarettes and the impact on health, the regulation of the products and financial implications. The Committee received over 100 pieces of written evidence and heard from 25 witnesses over the course of five oral evidence sessions held between January and May 2018. It published its report in August 2018. All seven of the recommendations made in the report – which covered matters such as addressing gaps in the evidence base on the health risks of e-cigarettes, and ensuring that NHS mental health trusts have clear, evidence-based policies on the use of e-cigarettes by patients – were subsequently accepted by the Government.

12 January 2022

'Beside himself with craving': the teenagers hooked on vaping

One mother says son loved mountain biking but a year later 'he's not interested – he runs out of breath'.

By Clea Skopeliti

When Sarah caught her 13-year-old son vaping in his room last year, he tried a classic teenage line on her. 'He said: "It's not mine, it's my friend's,"' remembers the teacher from West Yorkshire. 'I said: "Yeah, pull the other one, it's got bells on."'

Liam*, now 14, first tried vaping with two friends after one of them sneaked a parent's vape. 'They'd been watching videos on TikTok showing tricks you can do,' says Sarah. 'I think they thought it was cool.'

Between 2021 and 2022, the proportion of 11- to 17-year-olds in Britain who vape rose from 3.3% to 7%, according to Action on Smoking and Health (Ash). The proportion of those who had tried vaping increased from 11.2% to 15.8%.

A year on, Sarah describes her son as 'completely addicted'. When she first caught him vaping, she 'dropped down on him really hard'. 'We grounded him and took everything off him,' she says. He told her he didn't realise it was addictive; he thought he'd be able to stop easily.

But a month later he was caught stealing a vape. She was 'disgusted' and made him pay the shopkeeper back and write a letter of apology. Feeling 'backed into a corner', Sarah decided to change tack and buy him a refillable vape herself; she hopes she can support him to quit by reducing the strength of the e-liquid.

Liam still vapes every day. He tried to quit last October, announcing one morning that he had smashed up his vape and was going to stop. But when he got home from school that afternoon, he told his mother that he had had 'the worst day of his life'.

'He was just beside himself with craving,' says Sarah, adding he had begged her to go and buy him a vape. 'He just couldn't calm down – he was saying: "I'm never going to be able to stop." It broke my heart.'

Most experts agree that vaping carries far lower health risks than smoking, says Ann McNeill, professor of tobacco addiction at King's College London. 'Nicotine is an addictive substance but not the one that kills,' she says. But nuance is important: 'If you've got something very dangerous and something much less dangerous, it doesn't mean it's harmless.'

McNeill last year led an evidence review examining biomarkers of potential harm – measures of biological changes – due to vaping or smoking. 'The message from the data was that it's substantially less harmful than smoking, but not risk free. If you smoke, there's never going to be a situation when it won't be safer to vape, but if you've never smoked, don't take up the product.'

The rise of the disposable vape has been meteoric. In 2021, just 7.7% of teenage vapers used them; by 2022, this figure had jumped to 52%, according to Ash. Teenage smoking continues to decline, and for the first time in 2022, the majority of children who had tried vaping did so having never smoked.

McNeill acknowledges that 'disposables seem to be more attractive to the younger audience'. 'I think that is something we need to look at – if we are seeing "never smokers" taking up disposables, we need to make sure we're enforcing the law so that these products can't be sold quite so readily as they clearly are at the moment.'

Sarah says her son was able to buy vapes 'very easily'. 'He never got challenged – he is tall but there is no way he looks 18, he's got a baby face. He can't even get into a 15 at the cinema.'

Liam used to be 'mad into mountain biking' but he is 'just not interested now – he runs out of breath', Sarah says. He vapes throughout the day: on the way to school, in the toilets between every lesson, during breaks and on the way home.

It is a story that plays out in many secondary schools. Whereas before the summer holidays, Laura*, a secondary school teacher in Tyne and Wear, would catch a student vaping once a fortnight, lately it's an everyday occurrence: 'From about 13 upwards, many of them have vapes – as soon as they're out of the school gates they go in their pockets.'

Laura says she has noticed a change in students' behaviour in class. 'You can see when they're starting to get edgy before break time,' she says. 'They might get a bit snappy or angsty. They will then go to the toilets to vape because they haven't had any for two or three hours in lessons.'

The school has a zero-tolerance policy to vaping on the premises; when students are caught, the e-cigarettes are confiscated and parents or guardians are informed. She says the reaction from parents is mixed; while many are 'concerned and disappointed', some have the opposite reaction, 'giving [the vape] back to the student in front of us, and then the students tell us their parent bought the vape for them'.

'Students see it as the norm,' she explains. 'Their parents vape, their friends vape. If we're teaching about smoking, they say it's disgusting. They see [vaping] as a totally different thing.'

While he may have cadged the odd cigarette at a party, Dan, 19, has never been a smoker. The student from Cambridgeshire is angry about what he sees as vape companies angling their product towards teenagers. 'It's so clearly targeted to the younger generation,' he says. 'All the fruity flavours – someone who has been smoking for 20 years doesn't need a strawberry ice-cream vape. I don't know anybody who smokes.'

Dan started vaping at 17 after he and three friends bought disposable vapes for a party. 'We'd seen people doing it around school and wanted to try it. It was pure stupidity,' he says. 'All four of us [now] vape every day, for the past year and a half.'

He began vaping regularly soon after; he had no problem getting them from the corner shop. 'It just snowballed – I started buying them every time one died. I hate it so much, it's so difficult to quit. Among kids and teens it's such a big problem.'

These days, he goes through two or three disposable vapes a week. He has been trying to quit since January, but is finding it tough: it's just too easy to vape. 'It's constantly just there – say you smoke cigarettes, you're forced to go outside. When you vape, you can do it everywhere.'

Though he is concerned about the environmental impact, Dan has only ever used disposable vapes; he finds the flavours more appealing and the convenience hard to beat. 'I think they should be banned, to be honest,' he says. 'Banning them will force people like me to make a mental decision to buy a proper vape, or just stop. They have hooked the younger generation on nicotine.'

Names have been changed

18 March 2023

Research that implies vaping is a gateway to teenagers smoking is questioned by experts

Research that appeared in *Tobacco Control* this week, looked at teenagers who smoked cigarettes and concluded that if they also vaped they would be more likely to go on to smoke. In reaching a conclusion, the research looked at two different schools of thought: firstly the 'diversion' hypothesis that sees vaping use reducing the frequency of later cigarette use; and secondly 'catalyst' hypothesis, that predicts vaping use leads to smoking. It also cites research done in France that concludes the former theory – that vaping use reduces the frequency of cigarette smoking for teenagers.

I should stress at this point that, while the incidence of teenage use of vapes is relatively low, it is unacceptable for children to have access to vape products and the UKVIA has been campaigning for many years to strengthen the way retailers are policed in selling to teenagers. Progress is being made but it is our belief that more can be done. What is also critical is that we ensure parents and schools are given all the facts to help understand the facts around vaping, to deal with the wealth of misinformation out there today.

Action on Smoking and Health (ASH) conducted research in 2022 that included the finding that incidence of vaping amongst teenagers who hadn't previously smoked cigarettes was very low (0.5%), compared to those who had previously smoked (7%). The research published by Tobacco Control only looked at teenagers who had previously smoked; however, and perhaps crucially it is not clear, or rather the researchers are not clear, what comes first – vaping use or cigarette use. Experts writing for the Science Media Centre also pointed out that two key determinants of smoking in young people or adults were ignored – dependence and mental health. This is important for a number of reasons, not least as we know those who suffer from mental health problems find it harder to stop smoking and could therefore use vaping to deal with nicotine withdrawal in environments where they are not able to smoke cigarettes.

Dr Jamie Hartmann-Boyce, Associate Professor in Evidence-Based Policy and Practice, University of Oxford said:

'Although well-conducted, this type of study cannot prove that vaping causes young people to start smoking or to smoke more than they should have in the absence of e-cigarettes – a limitation acknowledged by the authors.'

Professor Peter Hajek, Director of the Tobacco Dependence Research Unit, Queen Mary University of London, said:

'If vaping led to smoking, we would see an increase in smoking rates among young people since vaping came along. In reality, the decline in smoking among young people has accelerated.'

As highlighted above, the UKVIA believes that no children should have access to vapes or be using vapes and more needs to be done. This also goes for the research, as the more we understand the facts about vape products, the better.

2023

Discuss

Hold a class discussion about why some young people are attracted to using e-cigarettes or vapes, even if they have never smoked tobacco before. Do you think this might lead them to start smoking cigarettes?

Australia bans recreational vaping to avoid having 'nicotine addicts'

E-cigarettes were not 'sold as a recreational product – especially not one for our kids,' says health minister.

By Maroosha Muzaffar

Australia has announced a ban on disposable vapes and decided to increase the tobacco tax by billions of dollars in the next few years.

Health minister Mark Butler laid out an ambitious plan to eliminate a rampant vaping black market amid concerns that a new generation of young people has become addicted to nicotine.

'Vapes contain more than 200 chemicals that do not belong in the lungs. Some of the same chemicals you will find in nail polish remover and weed killer,' Mr Butler said.

'This is a product targeted at our kids. Vaping has become the No. 1 behavioural issue in high schools, and it's becoming widespread in primary schools. This must end.'

Mr Butler said hard-won gains in public health pertaining to a reduction in smoking could be undone by the 'new threat'.

According to the *Sydney Morning Herald*, one in six teenagers between 14 and 17 years of age and a quarter of people between 18 and 24 years have vaped. It cited a recent study published in the *Australian and New Zealand Journal of Public Health*.

Mr Butler previously said there were as many as two million vapers in Australia.

The health minister, however, noted that for the vapes that remain legal when purchased with a doctor's prescription, further rules will apply. He said there will be restrictions on flavours and colours, pharmaceutical-like packaging and limited nicotine concentrations and volumes. There will also be a total ban on single-use, disposable products.

'No more bubblegum flavors. No more pink unicorns. No more vapes deliberately disguised as highlighter pens for kids to be able to hide them in their pencil cases,' he was quoted as saying by CNN.

Mr Butler said he would also make it easier for people to get a prescription for 'legitimate therapeutic use'.

Currently, according to local media, there are a limited number of doctors willing to prescribe vapes as a smoking cessation tool.

'Vaping was sold to governments and communities around the world as a therapeutic product to help long-term smokers quit,' he said.

'It was not sold as a recreational product – especially not one for our kids. But that is what it has become: the biggest loophole in Australian history.'

'Just like they did with smoking, Big Tobacco has taken another addictive product, wrapped it in shiny packaging and added flavours to create a new generation of nicotine addicts. This must end.'

The country's tax on tobacco will be increased as well. The tax will be raised by 5 per cent a year starting this September.

This will amount to a total increase of AU$3.3 billion ($2.2 billion) over four years.

It follows an AU$234 million ($157 million) boost for tougher regulation of e-cigarettes, including new controls on their importation and packaging.

2 May 2023

Debate

As a class, debate whether or not vapes should be available on prescription only to smokers who are trying to quit.

Does vaping really damage DNA and increase the risk of cancer?

An article from The Conversation.

By Caitlin Notley, Senior Lecturer in Mental Health, University of East Anglia and Konstantinos Farsalinos, Research Associate, University of West Attica, Greece

Vapers experience DNA changes, according to a recent paper published in Nature, and the changes are similar to those seen in smokers – although much less pronounced.

Crucially, this evidence was based on a few people by examining changes in their DNA at the time of the analysis, similar to creating a snapshot image, without considering any potential future change in vaping or smoking behaviour. The study does not provide real-world evidence of vaping-associated ill health in humans.

Positively, the study attempts to separate the effects of vaping itself from the effects of damage caused by tobacco smoking. This is difficult because most vapers use e-cigarettes to help them stop smoking and so are likely to be ex-smokers.

An important outcome of this analysis, somewhat buried in the paper, is that the damaged genes in smokers was about 7.4 times higher than in vapers. So what this study finds is what we know already: vaping is not completely risk free but is much less risky than smoking tobacco.

Transcriptomics (the study of 'gene readouts' in a cell), which this study used, is a promising field that explores the molecular mechanisms and potential processes leading to the future development of cancer. However, it cannot currently be used to accurately predict future cancer risk.

The study recruited a relatively small number of people who were not representative of the population. And it did not consider other lifestyle habits that may affect the measurements, such as alcohol use.

Studies are already emerging showing that switching from smoking to e-cigarettes can have health benefits, such as improvement in respiratory symptoms and lung function in asthma patients, or improvements in measurements that predict the future development of disease, such as blood vessel function for cardiovascular disease.

Other studies show that exposure to toxins is far lower in vapers who used to smoke compared with current smokers. It is important to look at all the evidence, which supports the harm reduction role of e-cigarettes as a smoking substitute.

Sadly, studies that do not examine direct clinical effects are easily interpreted and reported as evidence of health damage. A Daily Mail headline states: 'Vaping damages DNA and raises the risk of cancer the same way as cigarettes'. Although the second part of the headline offers balance: 'but it's not as bad as traditional smoking', the damage to public perceptions may already be done.

Nothing is risk free

No one is claiming that e-cigarettes are completely risk free. Inhaling anything into the lung may result in changes to DNA that could increase risks for future disease. Inhaling fumes from diesel cars, for example, has been shown to cause DNA changes. For the public good, the focus should be on reducing harm, since preventing all harm is impossible.

Many people are physically dependent on nicotine. People may come to first use nicotine through smoking tobacco, or, less commonly, may start using nicotine by vaping. Once dependent, it is very hard to quit. If you try to stop, you will suffer from unpleasant withdrawal symptoms and experience cravings.

Some people, particularly with support, can overcome nicotine dependence. Others find it more difficult or don't want to stop using nicotine. For these people, public health doctors must encourage smokers to use nicotine in ways that reduce harm, through vaping or by using nicotine replacement products.

The costs to people's health of using nicotine by continuing to smoke are huge. The World Health Organization estimates that tobacco kills more than 8 million people a year.

It is irresponsible to report sensationalist headlines to the public based on complex studies that in reality do not show any real-world harm. Particularly compared to the immense harms to health of tobacco smoking.

6 December 2021

Research

In small groups, have a look at some recent headlines about vaping. How many are 'sensationalist'?

Re-write the headline to make it more accurate. Does it have the same impact on readers?

THE CONVERSATION

Rise of single-use vapes sending tonnes of lithium to landfill

By Matthew Chapman

Millions of disposable vapes that could be recycled are ending up in landfill despite containing lithium, an in-demand metal needed for batteries.

A joint investigation by the Bureau, Sky News and the *Daily Telegraph* suggests that two disposable vapes are being thrown away every second in the UK. Over a year, this is enough lithium to make roughly 1200 electric car batteries.

Sales of disposable vapes are currently booming. A survey by Opinium – on behalf of Material Focus, a not-for-profit recycling organisation – found 18% of 4,000 people surveyed had bought a vape in the previous year, with 7% buying a single-use device. Having virtually disappeared, disposable vapes now appear to be driving the growth in the overall e-cigarette market.

The Opinium figures would suggest about 168 million disposable vapes are being bought every year in the UK. Two of the biggest brands in the country are Elf Bar and Geek Bar, which between them make up about 60% of the market. Most of the devices, also known as single-use e-cigarettes, contain a rechargeable battery but no charging port and are designed to be disposed of once the battery runs out.

More than half of people that buy single-use vapes bin them, according to the research.

While each vape contains just 0.15g of lithium, the scale of the waste means about 10 tonnes of the metal is ending up in landfills.

'We can't be throwing these materials away. It really is madness in a climate emergency – lithium is one of the things that is going to fuel the green economy,' Mark Miodownik, professor of materials and society at University College London, said. 'It's in your laptop, it's in your mobile phone, it's in electric cars. This is the material that we are absolutely relying on to shift away from fossil fuels. We need to take care of every bit of lithium.'

Lithium demand for batteries is forecast to increase fivefold by 2030, according to one industry consultant. Producing the metal is a complex process that uses huge amounts of energy and water.

In the UK, vapes are classified as waste electrical and electronic equipment (WEEE) and require specialist recycling.

Importers bear certain obligations for electrical and electronic waste and should be listed on the public register under WEEE producer requirements. The Bureau could find no evidence of the importers of Elf Bar and Geek Bar on the register, nor that they take any specific steps to promote recycling. Elf Bar and Geek Bar did not respond to requests for comment.

'The challenge is somebody looks at [a vape] and doesn't really think about what it's made of, they think about what it does for them,' said Scott Butler, executive director of Material Focus.

Disposable vapes also pose a potential serious risk when not recycled, as the lithium-ion batteries can start fires when crushed in a waste truck or at a waste-processing plant. 'They can [catch fire] very fast and very hard, and if they go in the back of a waste vehicle, which they have done, that waste is fuel for that fire,' Butler said.

Disposable vapes come in a range of flavours, including blueberry bubblegum and watermelon, and appeal particularly to young people.

'As we came out of the first lockdown, Geek Bar became really popular,' Dom Nguyen, an employee at a vape shop in Soho, London, said. 'We were getting requests for these particular Geek Bars and then eventually all vape shops were stocking the device and there were shortages ... It caused a craze because when you can't get something, you want more of it.'

Office for National Statistics data from 2020 found that 6.4% of people in the UK vape, while another 7.8% had tried vaping.

Sheila Duffy, chief executive of the charity Action on Smoking and Health Scotland, said: 'Disposable e-cigarettes are of particular concern as these products are designed exclusively for single use and the size of the market has increased exponentially during the last year, especially due to their popularity with younger people.'

The charity is calling for a Holyrood review to consider if 'regulatory action is needed to address the risks of any ecological damage' from disposable vapes.

A spokesperson for the Department for Environment, Food and Rural Affairs said it will be exploring improvements to the collection and recycling of electronic equipment this year.

15 July 2022

Key Facts

- Two disposable vapes are being thrown away every second in the UK.
- Roughly 168 million disposable vapes are being bought every year in the UK.
- 10 tonnes of the metal lithium is ending up in landfills every year.

www.thebureauinvestigates.com

Vaping substantially less harmful than smoking, largest review of its kind finds

New research from the Institute of Psychiatry, Psychology & Neuroscience (IoPPN) at King's College London has found that the use of vaping products rather than smoking leads to a substantial reduction in exposure to toxicants that promote cancer, lung disease and cardiovascular disease.

New research from the Institute of Psychiatry, Psychology & Neuroscience (IoPPN) at King's College London has found that the use of vaping products rather than smoking leads to a substantial reduction in exposure to toxicants that promote cancer, lung disease and cardiovascular disease.

The independent report, commissioned by the Office for Health Improvement and Disparities in the Department of Health and Social Care, represents the most comprehensive review of the risks of vaping to date. It found that, while vaping is not risk free (particularly for people who have never smoked), it poses a small fraction of the health risks of smoking in the short to medium term.

The report reviewed many aspects of vaping, including who is vaping and what products, the effects on health (both absolute and compared with smoking) and public perceptions of harm. The authors examined studies of biomarkers of exposure (measures of potentially harmful substance levels in the body) as well as biomarkers of potential harm (measures of biological changes in the body) due to vaping or smoking.

The strongest evidence, and where there was a greater volume of research, came from biomarkers of exposure. An exploration of the available studies found that levels of tobacco specific nitrosamines, volatile organic compounds and other toxicants implicated in the main diseases caused by smoking were found at significantly lower levels in vapers. Among vapers, overall levels of nicotine were lower or similar to smokers.

> **'The levels of exposure to cancer causing and other toxicants are drastically lower in people who vape compared with those who smoke. Helping people switch from smoking to vaping should be considered a priority if the Government is to achieve a smoke-free 2030 in England.'** – Dr Debbie Robson, a Senior Lecturer in Tobacco Harm Reduction King's IoPPN and one of the report's authors

When comparing biomarkers between people who vape and people who don't smoke or vape, they were often similar, but in some cases there was higher exposure when vaping. The investigators therefore concluded that whilst less harmful than smoking, vaping is likely to sustain some risks particularly for people who have never smoked.

While the investigators are clear on the benefits of vaping vs smoking, they found that public perceptions are lagging behind. In 2021, only 34% of adults who smoked accurately perceived that vaping was less harmful than smoking, while only 11% of adult smokers knew that nicotine wasn't the primary cause of the health risks connected to smoking tobacco.

Key Fact

- In 2021, only 34% of adults who smoked accurately perceived that vaping was less harmful than smoking, while only 11% of adult smokers knew that nicotine wasn't the primary cause of the health risks connected to smoking tobacco.

Vaping is seeing increasing popularity among adults. According to the latest data from the Action on Smoking and Health (ASH) Smokefree GB Adult survey, current vaping prevalence is 8.3% in 2022, compared with 7.1% in 2021 and 6.3% in 2020.

Vaping has also increased among young people. Data from the ASH Smokefree GB Youth survey of 11-to 18-year-olds in England show that current vaping prevalence (including occasional and regular) is 8.6% in 2022, compared with 4.0% in 2021 and 4.8% in 2020. Use of disposable vaping products has increased substantially over the last year. Vaping among young people who have never smoked remains very low at 1.7%.

> 'Smoking is uniquely deadly and will kill one in two regular sustained smokers, yet around two-thirds of adult smokers, who would really benefit from switching to vaping, don't know that vaping is less harmful. However, the evidence we reviewed indicates that vaping is very unlikely to be risk-free. So we strongly discourage anyone who has never smoked from taking up vaping or smoking.'– Professor Ann McNeill, a professor of tobacco addiction at King's IoPPN and the report's lead author

Dr Jeanelle DeGruchy, Deputy Chief Medical Officer for England, said, 'Every minute someone is admitted to hospital in England due to smoking. Every eight minutes someone dies a smoking-related death. This important study is the latest in a series which carefully pulls together the science on vaping to help reduce the damage from smoking.

'Vaping is substantially less harmful than smoking so the message is clear, if the choice is between smoking and vaping, choose vaping. If the choice is between vaping and fresh air, choose fresh air. Quitting smoking is one of the best things you can do for your health, please give it a go this Stoptober.'

29 September 2022

Passive vaping: an impending threat to bystanders

An article from The Conversation.

By Beladenta Amalia, Doctoral Researcher in Public Health, Universitat de Barcelona

Electronic cigarettes (e-cigarettes), also known as vapes, are gaining popularity among youths in many parts of the world, including the US and Europe.

These young vapers are often unaware their e-cigarettes contain nicotine, an addictive substance that is also present in tobacco cigarettes.

Little do vapers know that their habit may also endanger non-vapers. Vapers may expose others to e-cigarette emissions.

The danger of passive vaping

Passive vaping, or secondhand exposure, is a condition where bystanders, usually non-vapers, are exposed to the exhaled aerosol from e-cigarette use.

Unlike passive smoking, which includes the smoke released from the end of the burning cigarette (side stream), passive vaping only comes from the exhaled e-cigarette aerosol since the device does not yield side stream.

Passive vaping is as concerning as passive smoking for at least two reasons.

1. E-cigarette aerosol from passive vaping contains dangerous toxins

Vaping aerosols do not only contain water vapour as commonly believed.

The toxins include, among others, fine and ultra-fine particles (also known as particulate matter), nicotine, volatile organic compounds like formaldehyde and acetaldehyde, as well as metals. The latter was found in e-cigarette aerosol at a higher level than in tobacco smoke.

Formaldehyde and acetaldehyde can cause cancer in humans. Nicotine may cause impaired brain function, especially in young people.

The particulate matter is smaller in e-cigarette aerosol than is found in cigarette smoke. This makes it easier for these particles to penetrate the lungs and induce diseases such as cardiovascular and respiratory diseases and diabetes.

Many studies show levels of particulate matter and nicotine increase in an indoor environment during and after vaping, suggesting it creates indoor pollution.

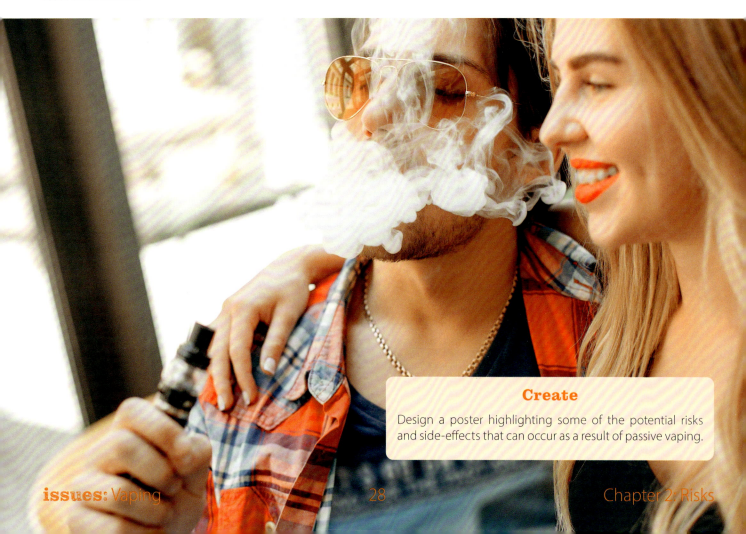

Create

Design a poster highlighting some of the potential risks and side-effects that can occur as a result of passive vaping.

For example, in homes of e-cigarette users, the concentration of indoor airborne nicotine was more than six times higher than in non-users' homes.

People who lived with vapers also absorbed the nicotine from the aerosol into their system.

Airborne nicotine and fine particulate matter from passive vaping may also contaminate other rooms or spaces as they can travel to neighbouring areas and outdoor environments.

The aerosol from passive vaping also contains other chemicals not present in regular cigarettes, such as propylene glycol and glycerol, which serve as the solvent in vape liquid, and flavourings.

Although propylene glycol and glycerol are considered safe for ingestion, they have not proved safe for inhalation.

Short-term exposure to e-cigarette aerosol has been shown to irritate eyes and airways and worsen respiratory conditions, such as asthma and chronic obstructive pulmonary disease, like chronic bronchitis.

This COVID-19 pandemic may put bystanders exposed to e-cigarettes at higher risk of contracting or having poor outcomes for COVID-19 since the aerosol may compromise lung function and immunity.

2. Passive vaping may endorse social acceptance of vaping and renormalise smoking

Studies found that youth seeing someone else vaping or exposed to the vaping aerosol were likely to initiate vaping or even smoking combustible cigarettes.

They even tend to perceive vaping or passive vaping as safe.

This raises concern about the gateway effect for non-smokers who may become smokers at a later stage or become dual users who vape and smoke.

Passive vaping is around us

The magnitude of passive vaping is not negligible. Exposure to e-cigarette aerosol has been pervasive, especially in countries where e-cigarette use is prevalent, like Greece and England .

In 2017-2018, 16% of adult bystanders in 12 European countries were exposed to e-cigarette aerosol in indoor settings.

In the US, passive vaping in indoor or outdoor public places was reported by nearly one in three middle and high-school students in 2018.

Indeed, passive vaping disproportionately affected youth, men and former vapers.

In Europe, passive vaping commonly occurred in places where smoking was already banned, including the indoor areas of bars, restaurants and workplaces or education facilities.

Vaping was even observed in locations where kids are likely around, such as children's playgrounds and school gates.

Recommendations

To mitigate the negative impacts of passive vaping on bystanders, we must closely monitor the trend of passive vaping in the population, especially among vulnerable groups such as children and people with threatening diseases.

Policymakers should consider including vaping in smoke-free policies to simplify communication and implementation of the regulations.

The WHO Framework Convention on Tobacco Control has advised countries to forbid vaping in enclosed spaces or at least in smoke-free places.

However, less than 60% of WHO European region countries had national laws on e-cigarette use by 2018.

This lack of regulation of e-cigarette aerosol occurs because European countries still focus more on other e-cigarette regulatory domains, such as marketing, retailing, pricing and product standards.

Fortunately, people are mainly in favour of vaping bans in public places, particularly in smoke-free areas. This implies an opportunity for authorities to adopt vaping regulations as part of the country's tobacco control strategy.

8 April 2021

THE CONVERSATION

The above information is reprinted with kind permission from The Conversation.
© 2010-2023, The Conversation Trust (UK) Limited

www.theconversation.com

Going up in smoke – how bad is vaping for the environment?

By Maxwell Marlo

- **Vaping is still far more environmentally friendly than smoking**

- **There are legitimate reasons to worry about the effect of discarded vapes**

- **The industry has come up with a viable solution to the battery issue**

Another day, another ban. Now the Government is taking aim at the most effective anti-smoking tool ever devised – disposable vapes. Alongside claiming that adults would not be so childish as to enjoy the taste of cola, fruits, or mint, the Government have highlighted the environmental concerns of disposable vapes. This may be a more valid concern than the phoney health argument. However, the industry has already begun innovating their way out of this quagmire.

To go back to basics, disposable vapes use lithium-ion batteries to power a metal coil, which heats a tank of glycerine, nicotine, and flavouring (all of which are non-carcinogenic). Shrouded in plastic, usually polycarbonate, when the tank is exhausted, the vape is usually thrown away, at a rate of two a second, into general waste or simply littered.

This does indeed entail some serious environmental problems.

Firstly, lithium-ion batteries contain cobalt, nickel, and manganese, which are poisonous if they make their way into soil or groundwater. That's to say nothing of the carbon and mineral-intensive production of the tens of millions of batteries produced each year for the vaping industry. Fortunately, that same industry has come up with a solution for the improper disposal of batteries. The Blo-Bar Disposable Vape Recycling Scheme allows users to send in 10 used vapes for proper recycling, and receive one for free. Likewise, Riot E-Liquids hosts an interactive map to help users find recycling centres around their towns and cities.

Secondly, and perhaps more importantly, vaping is still far more environmentally friendly than smoking. Not only do cigarettes release 7,000 chemicals when they are burned, but have you ever thought about what happens to the discarded butts you see scattered across our pavements? When in contact with water, or ground into the dirt by cars and foot-traffic, those same chemicals, which contain heavy metals such as aluminium, cadmium, chromium, copper, lead, mercury, nickel, and zinc, enter the environment. It goes without saying that these are terrible for the health of our soils and rivers. This includes the single-use plastics found in the filters of cigarette butts – industry has yet to integrate the dozens of biodegradable plastic filters and papers into their main product lines. With 18.5 billion butts disposed of every day, mostly discarded into the street, there's every reason to be concerned about their impact on the planet.

The argument, then, comes down to the trade-off. So long as people want nicotine, which is up to them, they will either smoke or vape or use pouches; as the Khan Review has highlighted, safer forms of nicotine consumption are the preference for public health. It is down to proper regulations, which reward innovative recycling and disposal methods and punish needlessly polluting practices. For both the health of the British people, and the health of the planet, the Government should back vaping and ensure the industry has a sustainable future.

Maxwell Marlow is Director of Research at the Adam Smith Institute. Columns are the author's own opinion and do not necessarily reflect the views of CapX.

29 March 2023

Government 'risks harm' by not banning vapes

75 per cent of Britons support a ban on disposable vapes.

By Michele Theil

Campaigners fighting for a ban on disposable vapes and e-cigarettes have said the government is risking 'harm' to people's health and the environment by not taking immediate action.

Laura Young, an environmental campaigner who used Twitter to kickstart a campaign to #BanDisposableVapes, told the Big Issue: 'While the government delays and risks more harm to young people's health, to waste workers at risk from battery-induced fires, and to the environment, we will continue to raise awareness of the many consequences of these harmful products.'

Young's response came after environment minister Rebecca Pow said there is 'no immediate plan to ban disposable vapes' after another Conservative MP suggested they should be included in the ban on single-use plastics starting in October.

Pow added the government would 'consult on policies aimed at driving up levels of separate collection of electric and electronic waste, including vaping devices' as part of separate legislation later in the year.

Young said it was 'extremely disappointing and frustrating that the UK government is unwilling to look into the impact single-use disposable vapes are having on both public health and the environment'.

She has called for an immediate ban across the UK, an action which would be supported by 75 per cent of Britons, according to a recent YouGov survey.

While the long-term health risks of vapes are still unknown, studies have found they cause similar damage to the body as cigarettes, if on a smaller scale.

The plastic, nicotine, and lithium-based batteries present in nearly all disposable vapes present environmental problems, as the batteries have been found to start fires in waste disposal centres and pollute the environment.

An estimated 68 million disposable vapes are thrown away each year in the UK.

Young praised a review commissioned by the Scottish government and led by Zero Waste Scotland that will look at banning disposable vapes and examine how other countries have dealt with the product. The Westminster government should follow suit, she said.

A Defra spokesperson told the Big Issue: 'All electrical waste should be properly disposed of and recycled to protect our environment – this includes disposable vape pens.

Key Facts

- 75 per cent of Britons support an immediate ban on single-use disposable vapes.
- An estimated 68 million disposable vapes are thrown away each year in the UK.
- Nearly 10 tonnes of lithium is being thrown away each year in disposable vapes – enough to make batteries for 1,200 electric cars.

'Our Environmental Improvement Plan sets out our plan to review rules for the collection and recycling of waste electricals this year. As part of this, we will consider what changes in legislation are needed to ensure the vaping sector foots the bill for the collection and treatment of their used products.'

Libby Peake, head of resource policy at Green Alliance, also supported a ban. She told the Big Issue: 'There's no reason these throwaway vapes should exist – for the health of the planet and future generations, the government must ban them.'

Green Alliance joined the Marine Conservation Society, the RSPCA, the Royal College of Paediatrics and Child Health, and 14 other environment and health groups in signing an open letter in November calling for environment secretary Thérèse Coffey and health secretary Steve Barclay to ban disposable vapes.

Peake also pointed out that vapes contain lithium and copper, 'which are vital to low carbon technologies'.

'It's a scandal that they are being squandered in throwaway e-cigarettes,' she added.

Nearly 10 tonnes of lithium is being thrown away each year in disposable vapes according to the *Bureau of Investigative Journalism* – enough to make batteries for 1,200 electric cars.

No country has yet banned the use of disposable vapes specifically, though the Irish government has also been looking into the impact of the product through a public consultation.

27 March 2023

Is lung inflammation worse in e-cigarette users than smokers, as a new study suggests?

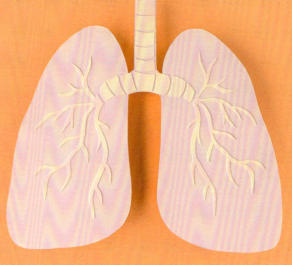

An article from The Conversation.

By Aaron Scott, Associate Professor in Respiratory Science, University of Birmingham and Shaun Thein, Clinical Lecturer in Respiratory Medicine, University of Birmingham

A small study that compared the lungs of cigarette smokers with e-cigarette smokers found that e-cigarette smokers had more lung inflammation than those who smoked tobacco. The pilot study, published in *The Journal of Nuclear Medicine*, is the first to use PET imaging to compare smokers' lungs with vapers' lungs.

E-cigarettes are now much more than 'new smoking cessation tools', they are big business. The global e-cigarette or 'vape' market value has increased from US$1.7 billion in 2013 (£1.4 billion) to an estimated all-time high of US$24.6 billion in 2022 (£20.8 billion). This massive increase in sales reflects an increase in usage beyond the ex-smoker market. Youth uptake is also at an all-time high. Current figures suggest one in ten middle-to high-school students in the US uses an e-cigarette.

Understanding the effects that e-cigarettes have on the lungs is essential for doctors to prepare for the future. Tobacco cigarettes were originally regarded as an aid to a healthy lifestyle. This poor understanding persisted while scientific evidence battled with economic interest from big tobacco companies, before the actual devastating effects of smoking were revealed decades too late. This same economic interest persists today, so it is vital for scientists to examine all the emerging evidence to ensure history does not repeat itself.

Many of the studies of e-cigarettes have so far looked at the effects of the vapour on immune cells in vitro (in a dish). These experiments show that immune cells that are normally involved in inflammation don't function as they should, which might cause damage to the lungs.

Macrophages, immune cells that are in human lungs and help to digest bacteria and regulate inflammation, have been shown to cause more inflammation when exposed to e-cigarette vapour.

This latest pilot study, from researchers at the University of Pennsylvania, examined lung inflammation in people who have vaped, those who smoked cigarettes, and non-smokers. They used positron emission tomography (PET) imaging to examine the participants' lungs. This involves using 'tracer molecules', and is usually used in cancer diagnosis.

In this case, the tracer targeted an enzyme called inducible nitric oxide synthase, or iNOS. This enzyme is involved in the production of nitric oxide in the body – a gas that triggers inflammation. People with asthma and chronic obstructive pulmonary disease (COPD) have high levels of inflammation and iNOS.

Participants inhale the tracer, which binds to the enzyme. This can then be detected by the radioactivity receiver. Following this, images can be compared to determine how much tracer has bound in the lungs of smokers, vapers and non-smokers.

Significantly higher levels

The researchers found significantly higher levels of iNOS in e-cigarette smokers compared with both non-smokers and those who smoked normal cigarettes.

They also looked at blood markers of inflammation but found no difference between the groups. These results suggest that inflammation specifically in the lungs is worse in e-cigarette smokers than non-smokers and even those who smoke regular cigarettes.

But how robust are these findings?

For a start, this was a small study. There were five e-cigarette users, five cigarette smokers, and five people who had never smoked cigarettes or e-cigarettes. Larger studies are needed to replicate these findings and provide more robust statistics.

Also, e-cigarette use is very different between people. The liquid can be of different flavours and can contain varying concentrations of the chemicals used to create the vapour clouds. Different devices heat to different temperatures. And unlike tobacco cigarettes, scientists don't have a way to measure how much someone vapes. All this means that the five e-cigarette users could be extremely heavy users or very light users.

Despite these limitations, the study shows that the effects of e-cigarette vapour on immune cells does lead to inflammation in the lungs, with even higher levels of inflammation than for tobacco cigarette smokers. This is against the current weight of evidence suggesting lower levels of harm in vaping compared with smoking. More important here is the take-home message that e-cigarette smoking might harm human lungs in the long term, based on the short-term danger signals shown in this study.

Write

Write a couple of paragraphs outlining the pros and cons of vaping. Consider both the health and environmental issues in your piece.

Doing harm to prevent a greater harm

The usefulness of e-cigarettes is a more complex issue. Some treatments given to cancer patients cause harm to healthy parts of the body while helping fight the cancer. It is a cost-benefit analysis to decide if the benefit is worth the harm associated with use.

E-cigarettes may also cause harm but could still be recommended for the right people and the right reasons. E-cigarettes are being used to help people stop tobacco smoking. When we compare the chances of getting smoking-related diseases like COPD and cancer in people who smoke tobacco cigarettes compared with e-cigarettes, the rates are lower.

Using e-cigarettes to quit smoking seems like the right first step. Yet, as we don't know what problems might be caused by using e-cigarettes for long periods, this should not be the last step on the journey for smokers. Quitting nicotine altogether should be the end goal to ensure long-term health.

8 March 2023

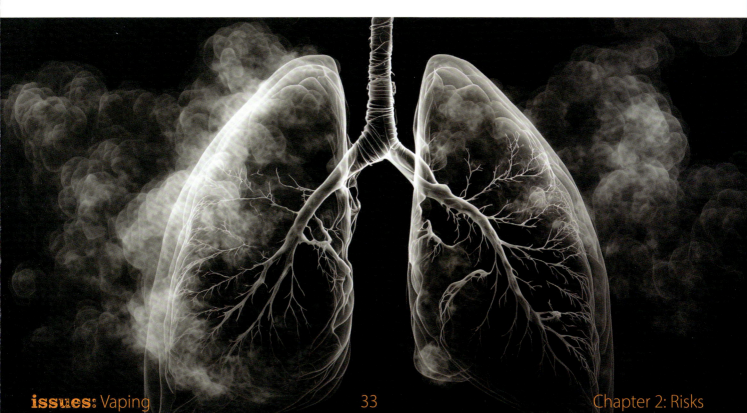

What next?

UK mulls new tax on vaping

Move comes amid surging use by children – but could prompt
a clash with Scotland.

By Emilio Casalicchio

LONDON – U.K. ministers are considering slapping a new tax on vaping products to discourage their use as part of a wider crackdown on the addictive smoking alternative.

Proposals being considered by the government also include regulations on packaging, marketing and flavorings in a bid to stem the increased use of vapes among children, two people with knowledge of the plans told POLITICO's Playbook PM.

Ministers are not, however, expected to impose an all-out ban on disposable vapes – teeing up a potential constitutional clash with the Scottish government if it goes down that route.

The proposals are being drawn up in response to the Khan review, which was published in 2022 and looked at whether the British government can make England smoking-free before 2030.

The government's response is set to be published in the spring and could include new legislation to tackle a surge in the use of vapes among young people, while also recognizing their benefits as a smoking cessation aid.

One person in the health department with knowledge of the discussions said: "We will be responding to the Khan Review some time in the Spring. It will look at vaping, with the benefits it has for getting people to stop smoking. Obviously, when it comes to kids vaping, we do have to nip that in the bud."

A Department of Health and Social Care spokesperson said in a statement: "We have strong regulations in place to prevent children from vaping. The law protects children from e-cigarettes through restricting sales to over 18s only, limiting nicotine content, refill bottle and tank sizes, labelling requirements and through advertising restrictions. Adverts for e-cigarettes and their components are prohibited from featuring anything likely to be of particular appeal to people under the age of 18, such as characters or celebrities would be familiar with."

"We are carefully considering the recommendations from the Khan Review, including what more can be done to protect children from vaping," the statement said.

Earlier this week England's Chief Medical Officer Chris Whitty told a House of Commons committee that vape marketing to children holds "unknown consequences for developing minds" and branded such targeting "an appalling situation." The rate of vaping among children had, he warned, doubled in the last couple of years.

But while the U.K. government is not considering a ban on disposable vapes, the devolved Scottish government has already said it will consider one.

Last month, Scottish health minister and now-Scottish National Party leadership hopeful Humza Yousaf said a government review would include "consideration of a potential ban."

That could tee up a constitutional tussle between the governments in Westminster and Holyrood.

Under the terms of the U.K.'s Internal Market Act, Holyrood could ban the manufacture and sale of the products in Scotland, yet be forced to allow them through the border from England.

The SNP's Scotland spokesperson at Westminster, Philippa Whitford, told Playbook PM: "This is why the Internal Market Act drives a coach and horses through devolution. Before you even get to the practicality it will create a political clash. You'll already have the constitutional issue of whether it will be able to happen."

Andrew McDonald contributed reporting.

24 February 2023

A ban on vape flavours could see 1.5 million return to smoking

- **In a survey commissioned by the UKVIA, 1 in 3 vapers fear a ban will lead them back to conventional cigarettes, which could be close to 1.5 million former smokers**

- **83 per cent of vapers claim that flavoured vapes help them pack in their smoking habits**

One in three vapers fear a ban on flavoured devices and liquids will lead them back to cigarettes, which could see close to 1.5 million former smokers returning to their habit. This comes as Ministers are considering putting a stop to the sale of flavoured vapes, as they look at measures that could discourage youth vaping. But a poll of 2,000 adults who use vapes found 76 per cent only started to quit their smoking habit, and that eight in ten vapers (83 per cent) claim that flavoured vapes help them pack in their smoking habits.

While 27 per cent agree there is a real need to tackle youth vaping, nearly four in 10 (37 per cent) want more effective enforcement handed out to retailers who are selling them to children – rather than an outright ban on flavours.

John Dunne, Director General of the UK Vaping Industry Association, which commissioned the research, said: 'The research shows there is a reliance on vapes to help smokers quit – and flavours have a role to play. While we are supportive of attempts to eradicate youth smoking, having a ban on flavours could have a negative impact on those who are attempting to quit. Often with these types of policies trying to stamp out one problem can cause another, and it shows many adult vapers are concerned about what they are hearing from the Government.

'The survey has shown many fear such a change could lead them back to smoking, meaning nearly 1.5 million current vapers across the UK could return to conventional cigarettes, based on the number of adult vape users (4.3 million) reported by the Office of National Statistics last year'.

The research also revealed the most popular flavours amongst adult vapers were the very ones that the Government is looking to consider banning. Whilst strawberry is the nation's favourite overall, other fruity flavours dominate the top five – including blueberry, watermelon, cherry and raspberry. Many also cited some more unusual preferences like lychee, Earl Grey and even a Bloody Mary.

Tobacco and menthol flavourings were the most common ones quitters turned to, although 65 per cent didn't receive any advice on the best flavours to help them on their quest to give up smoking.

And 83 per cent think having this guidance would be an important part of the quitting journey. Within the separate poll of 1,000 smokers, conducted via OnePoll.com, it found 36 per cent are currently trying to reduce the amount they use cigarettes by increasing how much they vape. And 75 per cent of these are confident it will help them to be successful on their quitting journey.

Dunne added: 'It is important to offer those who are trying to quit smoking the appropriate advice, including flavours, to support them during the process. We know that going cold turkey is not an option for many, and it shows a considerable amount are having success with flavoured vapes to help reduce, and ultimately cut out, their reliance on cigarettes.'

In March the UKVIA presented proposals to the government to address youth vaping. In its hard hitting action plan the association called for:

- Retailers, including owners and directors, to face fines of up to £10,000 per instance if they are caught selling to minors

- A new national registration scheme for retailers – with only those that meet strict qualifying criteria able to sell vape products

- The introduction of the first ever national test purchasing scheme to constantly monitor retailers for sales to minors on an ongoing basis

- Funding from the fines and retailer registration scheme to be used to finance heightened enforcement by Trading Standards

The above information is reprinted with kind permission from UKVIA.

© 2023 UKVIA

www.ukvia.co.uk

Smokers urged to swap cigarettes for vapes in world first scheme

Pregnant women will also be offered financial incentives to help them quit as part of a sweeping package of measures to cut smoking rates in England.

From: Department of Health and Social Care and Neil O'Brien MP

One million smokers will be encouraged to swap cigarettes for vapes under a pioneering new 'swap to stop' scheme designed to improve the health of the nation and cut smoking rates.

As part of the world-first national scheme, almost 1 in 5 of all smokers in England will be provided with a vape starter kit alongside behavioural support to help them quit the habit as part of a series of new measures to help the government meet its ambition of being smokefree by 2030 – reducing smoking rates to 5% or less. Local authorities will be invited to take part in the scheme later this year and each will design a scheme which suits its needs, including deciding which populations to prioritise.

In a speech today, Health Minister Neil O'Brien will also announce that following the success of local schemes, pregnant women will be offered financial incentives to help them stop smoking. This will involve offering vouchers, alongside behavioural support, to all pregnant women who smoke by the end of next year.

The government will also consult on introducing mandatory cigarette pack inserts with positive messages and information to help people to quit smoking.

Additionally, there will be a crackdown on illicit vape sales as part of measures to stop children and non-smokers take up the habit – which is growing in popularity among young people.

Health Minister Neil O'Brien will say:

'Up to 2 out of 3 lifelong smokers will die from smoking. Cigarettes are the only product on sale which will kill you if used correctly.

'We will offer a million smokers new help to quit. We will be funding a new national "swap to stop" scheme – the first of its kind in the world. We will work with councils and others to offer a million smokers across England a free vaping starter kit.'

The new policies will deliver the government's 3 aims to help more adults quit smoking, stop children and non-smokers from taking up vaping, and using vaping as a tool for established adult smokers to quit.

For those who quit, the risk of heart attack is halved after one year of quitting, ultimately halving the likelihood of ending up in a hospital bed or worse.

Supporting more women to have a smokefree pregnancy will reduce the number of babies born underweight or underdeveloped with health problems requiring neonatal and ongoing care. It will also reduce the risk of miscarriage and stillbirth.

Cutting smoking rates reduces the number of smoking-related illnesses needing to be treated, in turn reducing the pressure on the NHS, helping to deliver on our priority to cut NHS waiting lists.

NHS figures for 2021 showed that 9% of 11 to 15 year old children used e-cigarettes, up from 6% in 2018.

In recognition of the sharp increase, Minister O'Brien will launch a call for evidence on youth vaping to identify opportunities to reduce the number of children accessing and using vape products – and explore where government can go further.

Working with enforcement agencies and learning from the government's work with Trading Standards on illicit tobacco, £3 million of new funding will also be provided to create a specialised 'illicit vapes enforcement squad' to enforce the rules on vaping and tackle illicit vapes and underage sales.

As part of the measures, HMRC and Border Force will also be publishing an updated strategy this year to tackle illicit tobacco. It will lay out strategically how we continue to target, catch and punish those involved in the illicit tobacco market.

Smoking prevalence in England in 2021 was 13% – the lowest on record thanks to measures such as doubling duty on cigarettes since 2010 and continued funding to local stop smoking services.

In 2021 to 2022, £68 million of public health grant funding was spent on stop smoking services by local authorities and nearly 100,000 people quit with the support of a stop smoking service.

In addition, £35 million has been committed to the NHS this year so that all smokers admitted to hospital will be offered NHS-funded tobacco treatment services.

However, 5.4 million people in England smoke tobacco which remains the single biggest cause of preventable illness and death. Up to 2 out of 3 lifelong smokers will die from smoking and recent data shows 1 in 4 deaths from all cancers were estimated to be from smoking.

Last year an independent smoking review led by Javed Khan proposed a range of measures to help people stub out the addiction, which has informed the measures set out today.

11 April 2023

Key Facts

- In a world-first national scheme, 1 in 5 of all smokers in England will be provided with a vape starter kit and behavioural support to help them quit smoking

- In 2021 to 2022, £68 million of public health grant funding was spent on stop smoking services by local authorities and nearly 100,000 people quit with the support of a stop smoking service.

Waitrose becomes first UK supermarket to stop selling disposable vapes

By Matthew Chapman

Waitrose will stop selling disposable vapes following a Bureau investigation into the number of the devices that end up in landfill. The other 'big four' UK supermarkets either said they would continue selling the products or declined to respond to request for comment.

The Bureau approached Morrisons, Tesco, Sainsbury's and Asda to ask if they would stop selling single-use vaping products after Waitrose announced last month that it is completely withdrawing disposable vapes from its shelves. Tesco, Sainsbury's and Asda did not respond, while Morrisons said it does not plan to stop selling the products.

The environmental impact of disposable vapes was revealed in July by the Bureau in partnership with Sky News and the *Daily Telegraph*. Exclusive research showed that two devices were being binned every second in the UK, despite their batteries containing lithium, an in-demand metal that is vital to the green economy.

This means that 10 tonnes of lithium – enough for roughly 1,200 electric car batteries – is being sent to landfill each year just because of disposable vapes.

Waitrose cited this figure when it announced it was discontinuing the products and a spokesperson said the supermarket chain was 'very much aware of the [Bureau's] report' when making its decision.

Disposable vapes have become big business for supermarkets and Elf Bar is the fastest growing brand within the grocery sector, increasing its sales by £318.4 million in 2022, according to the Grocer. Morrisons, Tesco, Sainsbury's and Asda all sell either the Elf Bar or Geek Bar brands, which together make up an estimated 60% of the market.

A ban on disposable vapes is being considered by the Scottish government as part of a review being led by non-government organisation Zero Waste Scotland. This comes after lobbying from a coalition including ASH Scotland, campaigner Laura Young, Marine Conservation Society and Keep Scotland Beautiful.

The coalition has used the Bureau's data on disposable vapes in its e-cigarette waste briefing material.

Lorna Slater, the circular economy minister, said: 'Not only are single-use vapes bad for public health, they are also bad for the environment. We will consider the evidence and expert advice and come forward with policy options, which could include a potential ban on single-use vapes.

'In the meantime, we would urge everyone who uses these products to make sure they are disposed of properly.'

2 February 2023

Key Fact

- 10 tonnes of lithium – enough for roughly 1,200 electric car batteries – is being sent to landfill each year just because of disposable vapes.

Crackdown on illegal sale of vapes

Bold new measures to combat rising levels of youth vaping expected to be announced.

From: Department of Health and Social Care and Neil O'Brien MP

- **A new 'illicit vapes enforcement squad' – backed by £3 million of government funding – to be formed to enforce rules on vaping and tackle illegal sales of vapes to under 18s**

- **Call for evidence also launched to identify opportunities to stop children vaping**

The government is expected to unveil tough new measures to combat the illegal sale of vapes to under 18s as part of its plans to reduce smoking and tackle youth vaping.

In his speech at Policy Exchange on Tuesday 11 April, Health Minister Neil O'Brien is expected to announce a new 'illicit vapes enforcement squad' – backed by £3 million of government funding – to enforce the rules on vaping and tackle illicit vapes and underage sales.

Working across the country, the enforcement squad led by Trading Standards will share knowledge and intelligence across regional networks and local authorities.

It will undertake specific projects such as test purchasing in convenience stores and vape shops. It will also produce guidance to help build regulatory compliance, and will have the power to remove illegal products from shops and at our borders.

The minister is also expected to announce the launch of a call for evidence to identify opportunities to reduce the number of children accessing and using vapes, while ensuring they remain available as a quit aid for adult smokers.

It will explore topical issues such as the marketing and promotion of vapes and the environmental impact of disposable products.

Health Minister Neil O'Brien said:

'Smoking kills, so our priority is to prevent people smoking, and support them to quit. We remain committed to our ambition to be smokefree by 2030.

'However, while vaping is a preferable alternative to smoking for adults, we are concerned about the rise in youth vaping, particularly the increasing use of disposable vaping products.

'The new illicit vapes enforcement squad will work across the country and clamp down on those businesses who sell vapes to children – which is illegal – and get them hooked on nicotine. Our call for evidence will also allow us to get a firm understanding of the steps we can take to reduce the number of children accessing and using vapes.'

Smoking prevalence in England in 2021 was 13.0%, the lowest on record, thanks to measures such as doubling duty on cigarettes since 2010 and continued funding to local stop smoking services. In 2021 to 2022, £68 million of funding from the public health grant was spent on stop smoking services by local authorities, and nearly 100,000 people quit with the support of a stop smoking service.

In addition, £35 million was committed to the NHS last year so that all smokers admitted to hospital will be offered NHS-funded tobacco treatment services.

9 April 2023

Will an increase in youth vaping derail the UK's commitment to a smoke-free future?

By Dr. Nveed Chaudhary, Chief Scientific and Regulatory Officer at Broughton.

The last couple of months has seen the release of two key surveys highlighting a rise in youth vaping in the UK. This is important news not least because nobody wants to see an increase in the use of nicotine-based products by young people, but also because the UK regulatory authorities and politicians have taken a proactive approach in championing the benefits of next-generation nicotine delivery products (NGPs) to support tobacco harm reduction and help achieve the country's tobacco-free goals by 2030 (i.e., a national smoking rate of less than 5%).

If the UK is now experiencing an epidemic of 'youth vaping' as many media headlines have suggested, will the UK regulatory authorities need to revisit their pro-NGP position?

Do the media headlines tell the full story?

The Action on Smoking and Health (ASH) Survey – The Use of E-cigarettes by young people in Great Britain (published July 7, 2022) is based on survey data collected between March 1-29, 2022.

The annual YouGov youth survey on behalf of ASH showed that current vaping among children aged 11-17 increased from 4% in 2020 to 7% in 2022. The proportion of children who admit ever having tried vaping also rose from 14% in 2020 to 16% in 2022.

The results of the ASH Survey highlighted that disposable e-cigarettes are now the most used product among current vapers, up more than 7-fold from 7% in 2020 and 8% in 2021, to 52% in 2022. Elf Bar and Geek Bar are overwhelmingly the most popular brands, with only 30% of current users having tried any other brands.

However, ASH cautioned that although the increase in vaping shown by the survey is a cause for concern, 92% of under-18s who've never smoked have also never vaped, and only 2% have vaped more frequently than once or twice.

They also highlighted that use among 11-17-year-olds who have never smoked remains low and largely experimental. In contrast, 7.5% of never-smokers tried an e-cigarette in 2022 only 1.7% reported at least monthly use.

The NHS Survey Smoking, Drinking and Drug Use Among Young People in England, 2021 (published September 6, 2022) covered the survey date range from September 1, 2021, to February 28, 2022.

The 2021 survey was conducted by Ipsos Mori, and questioned 9,289 year 7 to 11 pupils, mostly aged 11 to 15. The majority (88%) of pupils were aware of e-cigarettes, and the survey showed the proportion of pupils classified as current e-cigarette users has increased from 6% in 2018 to 9% in 2021.

Pupils who had ever smoked were much more likely to have used an e-cigarette than those who had never smoked. 56% of ex-smokers were current e-cigarette users. Most regular smokers (92%) reported having ever used e-cigarettes. This compares to just 13% of pupils who had never smoked. Regular smokers who were regular e-cigarette users have more than doubled, from 29% in 2018 to 61% in 2021. Only 1% of pupils who had never smoked were regular e-cigarette users.

The Survey also highlighted that just three percent of students in the survey were classified as current smokers, meaning that both vaping and smoking in England are quite low.

Delving deeper into the youth vaping survey results

A more nuanced interpretation of the data gives interesting and powerful insights. A detailed reading of the NHS Survey illustrates that rather than introducing a new generation of youth to nicotine, vaping is helping young people who have already started smoking cigarettes to transition away from smoking tobacco. The increase in UK youth vaping is, to a large extent, mirrored by a decrease in youth smoking.

Therefore, rather than being a gateway to smoking cigarettes, for many UK youth, vaping is actually an off-ramping route. As The American Council on Science and Health (ACSH) points out 'This means that vaping, which is widely recognized as less harmful than smoking, has helped many young people replace some or all of their cigarette consumption.'

The ASH Survey results highlight a worrying increase in young people's misperception that e-cigarettes are more than or equally harmful than tobacco cigarettes. With only 42.1% of current 11-17-year-olds surveyed in 2022 believing that e-cigarettes were less harmful than cigarettes. Possibly this shows the damaging impact of negative headlines and a lack of evidence-based education around next generation products.

While the appeal of youth-friendly flavours and packaging continues to be a concern, the product's ready availability through small newsagents and convenience stores, as well as via mobile online purchases, are the biggest cause for concern. ASH highlights that from a total of 442 test purchases, using young people under the age of 18 years to attempt to purchase disposable vapes conducted in shops during February and March 2022, illegal sales were made on 145 occasions – a non-compliance rate of 33%. More concerning still is that a quarter of the purchased products did not meet UK regulatory standards and were not suitable for sale in the UK.

Enforcement of existing regulations

Alarmist media headlines and a lack of in-depth data analysis can create knee-jerk reactions and unhelpful calls to clamp down on vaping and e-cigarettes. While nobody

with a commitment to tobacco harm reduction wants to see youth vaping increase, if young cigarette smokers are moving away from tobacco towards vaping, as the evidence suggests, this surely strengthens the UK government's continued commitment to championing e-cigarettes to build a smoke-free future in the UK.

The UK already has a strong regulatory framework with the Tobacco and Related Products Regulations (TRPR), which needs to be fully enforced using all the power at the regulatory authorities' disposal. The Department of Health and Social Care (DHSC), the MHRA (Medical Health and Regulatory Authorities), and trading standards bodies must work together to ensure existing laws are upheld, and there are penalties for those that sell nicotine products to children. The UK Chartered Trading Standards Institute (CTSI) was commissioned to conduct a rapid review of retail compliance earlier in the year, and action must be taken to clamp down on both rogue traders and the illegal and non-compliant products they sell.

It is not more regulation that is needed in the UK to stop the growth in youth vaping but a detailed analysis of the causes and coordinated enforcement of the powers that already exist to prevent it. Looking beyond the recent headlines, the UK remains a beacon of hope for pragmatically establishing the principles of tobacco harm reduction to deliver a smoke-free future. Still, it must act now to ensure the gains it has made are not lost.

An alternative approach

One of the routes that has not been extensively explored by manufacturers is that of e-cigarettes as medicinal products in the UK. Aligned with the UK government's goal of achieving a smoke-free 2030, the MHRA is actively looking to approve e-cigarettes as nicotine replacement therapies. Products that receive a marketing order under a General Sales licence would be subject to the same sales restrictions as other general sale pharmaceutical products (e.g., paracetamol) and would use existing infrastructure and approved outlets to prevent youth access. Furthermore, if the manufacturer applies for a Pharmacy-Only licence, further restrictions on sales to minors can be guaranteed.

The MAA pathways for e-cigarettes provides an opportunity for manufacturers to market products higher than the current EU TPD limit of 20 mg/mL nicotine. Widespread understanding indicates that higher nicotine strengths provide a greater opportunity for heavy smokers to stop smoking combustible cigarettes. Manufacturers pursuing an MAA approval for e-cigarettes have the opportunity to bring to UK smokers, flavoured, high-concentration nicotine e-cigarettes, with a more controlled marketing infrastructure, limiting the access to youth and helping the UK achieve its 2030 smoke-free goal.

4 October 2022

Useful Websites

Useful Websites

www.ash.org.uk

www.bigissue.com

www.capx.co

www.commonslibrary.parliament.uk

www.gov.uk

www.independent.co.uk

www.kcl.ac.uk

www.medium.co.uk

www.metro.co.uk

www.openaccessgovernment.org

www.politico.eu

www.telegraph.co.uk

www.thebureauinvestigates.com

www.theconversation.com

www.theguardian.com

www.thejournalofmhealth.com

www.topdoctors.co.uk

www.ukvia.com

www.yougov.co.uk

Where can I find help?

Below are some telephone numbers, email addresses and websites of agencies or charities that can offer support or advice if you, or someone you know, needs it.

Asthma + Lung UK
Helpline: 0300 222 5800 (Monday to Friday, 9am to 5pm)
email helpline@asthmaandlung.org.uk
www.asthmaandlung.org.uk

British Lung Foundation
Helpline: 03000 030 555
www.lunguk.org

ASH (Action on Smoking and Health)
www.ash.org.uk

For more information and help with quitting smoking or vaping, visit your GP.

Further Reading

Page 7: Action on Smoking and Health (ASH). Use of e-cigarettes (vapes) among young people in Great Britain. 2022 Full report can be found here: https://ash.org.uk/uploads/Use-of-e-cigarettes-among-young-people-in-Great-Britain-2022.pdf

Page 27: Full report can be found here: https://www.gov.uk/government/publications/nicotine-vaping-in-england-2022-evidence-update

Glossary

Acetone

Widely used as a solvent, for example in nail polish remover, acetone is one of around 4,000 chemicals contained in the average cigarette. Also has been found in the vapour of some e-cigarettes.

Addiction

A dependence on a substance which makes it very difficult to stop taking it. Addiction can be either physical, meaning the user's body has become dependent on the substance and will suffer negative symptoms if the substance is withdrawn, or psychological, meaning a user has no physical need to take a substance, but will experience strong cravings if it is withdrawn.

Arsenic

A deadly poison used in insecticides, arsenic is contained in tobacco and is therefore inhaled during smoking. Arsenic has also been found in some vapes.

Brand

A product or service distinguished from other products, usually marketed with a distinctive name, logo and reputation.

Carcinogen

Any substance capable of causing cancer.

E-cigarette

A battery-operated device that is typically designed to resemble a traditional cigarette and is used to inhale a usually nicotine-containing vapour.

Elf bar

A hugely popular brand of disposable vape.

E-liquid

The substance used inside an e-cigarette, sometimes known as 'vape juice', that creates the vapour. E-liquids come in a wide range of flavours and nicotine strengths.

Formaldehyde

A chemical used to preserve corpses, Formaldehyde is contained in tobacco and some vapes.

Nicotine

An addictive chemical compound found in the nightshade family of plants that makes up about 0.6–3.0% of dry weight of tobacco. It is the nicotine contained in tobacco which causes smokers to become addicted, and many will use Nicotine Replacement Therapy such as patches, gum or electronic cigarettes to help them deal with cravings while quitting.

Nicotine replacement therapy (NRT)

NRT is a smoking cessation aid. It provides low-level nicotine without the tar, carbon monoxide and other toxic chemicals present in cigarette smoke. It is available over the counter or on prescription in patch, gum, lozenge, spray or inhaler form.

Passive smoking

Passive smoking refers to the inhalation of tobacco smoke by someone other than the smoker: for example, a parent smoking near their children may expose them to the poisonous chemicals in the second-hand smoke from their cigarette. This has been shown to have a negative impact on the passive smoker`s health.

Passive vaping

Passive vaping refers to the inhalation of e-cigarette vapour by someone other than the vaper/smoker.

Recycling

The process of turning waste into a new product. Recycling reduces the consumption of natural resources, saves energy and reduces the amount of waste sent to landfills.

The smoking ban

The Health Act 2006, which came into force in England and Wales on 1 July 2007, made it illegal to smoke in all enclosed public places and enclosed work places (similar bans were already in place in other parts of the UK). This has led to much debate about the balance between public health and individual freedoms.

Tobacco

Tobacco is a brown herb-like substance produced from the dried leaves of tobacco plants. The tobacco used in cigarettes contains many substances dangerous to the user when inhaled, including tar, which can cause lung cancer, and nicotine, which is highly addictive. Nevertheless, around 21 per cent of adults in the UK are smokers.

TPD

The TPD (Tobacco Products Directive) is a directive of the European Union which entered into force in 2014. It regulates the manufacture, presentation and sale of e-cigarettes, e-liquids and tobacco products.

Vaping

The inhalation through the mouth of a vapour created by the heating of a chemical liquid in an e-cigarette or other vaping device.

Index